The
Reiki
Healing
Handbook

Disclaimer

The Reiki Healing Handbook

Transmit healing energy through your hands
to achieve deep relaxation, inner peace,
and total well-being

Janet Green

CHARTWELL
BOOKS

Inspiring | Educating | Creating | Entertaining

Brimming with creative inspiration, how-to projects, and useful information to enrich your everyday life, Quarto Knows is a favorite destination for those pursuing their interests and passions. Visit our site and dig deeper with our books into your area of interest: Quarto Creates, Quarto Cooks, Quarto Homes, Quarto Lives, Quarto Drives, Quarto Explores, Quarto Gifts, or Quarto Kids.

© 2012 by Quantum Publishing Ltd.

This edition published in 2018 by Chartwell Books, an imprint of The Quarto Group,
142 West 36th Street, 4th Floor, New York, NY 10018, USA
T (212) 779-4972 **F** (212) 779-6058 **www.QuartoKnows.com**

10 9 8 7 6 5 4 3 2 1

ISBN: 978-0-7858-3601-8

Produced by Quantum Publishing Ltd.
The Old Brewery, 6 Blundell Street,
London N7 9BH

QUMTRHB

Assistant Editor: Jo Morley
Managing Editor: Samantha Warrington
Production Manager: Rohana Yusof
Publisher: Sarah Bloxham
Packaged by Gulmohur

Printed in China

While every effort has been made to credit contributors, Quantum would like to apologize should there have been any omissions or errors

The material in this book originally appeared in *The Reiki Healing Bible*.

Contents

Introduction

In 1992 I was living in London, working as a photographer in the fashion and music industries. This had been my goal since leaving college in 1983, and after a lot of hard work things were at last coming together. But despite my growing professional success, I had a nagging sense that something was missing from my life.

From my earliest childhood I had always been curious as to why I was here. I had been lucky enough to grow up in Africa, where the very closeness of nature instils a deep respect for all living things.

I was always happiest in the great outdoors. By contrast, I found London a difficult place to live in: deprived of horizons and sunsets, I felt truly cut off from nature. Looking back now at this sense of alienation I recognize that deep transformational forces were at work within me. Change was coming and I was powerless to stop it.

In early 1993 I had the first of a number of transcendental experiences. I was walking along a quiet road in a small town in the French Alps, having spent the evening with friends.

As I looked up at the winter night sky and saw a hundred billion stars twinkling, something shifted in me. It was as if I had caught a glimpse of my intimate connection with everything else in the universe. I felt enveloped in the warm glow of an overpowering love. This profoundly moving experience stayed with me for days.

On my return to London I knew that something inside me had changed forever. By chance I met a succession of people who had experienced this same sense of oneness. Soon I was swept up in a wave of New Age consciousness: this was a very confusing time for me and yet I felt sure it was right.

"How do you make God laugh? Tell him your plans."

Reawakening

Later that year I visited the Findhorn Community in Scotland, where I experienced a sense of communion so intense that it was at times almost too much to bear. I realized that I had spent years developing a hardness around my heart to enable me to function in the world. Suddenly it was breaking down: the flood gates were opening, and I could do nothing but surrender. Five days into my stay I was taken to a hill known as the Power Point, a place where many ley lines intersect. What occurred there threw my whole perception of reality into doubt: I experienced such powerful surges of physical energy that I felt as if I had been plugged into a power supply. My whole body vibrated with electricity; I found it almost impossible to breathe, and great sobs emanated from deep within me. Of our group, only I felt this energy, and I found this confusing. For a week or two I walked around with a messiah complex; then I began to worry about my state of mind. Finally, I tried to forget the whole thing.

But I couldn't put it out of my head. The next thing I knew, everyone I met seemed to be involved in healing in one way or another. I was hitchhiking and the person who picked me up turned out to be a healer. Or I got into conversation with someone in a bar and they'd just been to see a healer. Someone was trying hard to get my attention.

One day I noticed a woman sitting next to me on the bus holding her stomach and heart with her hands. Intrigued, I asked what she was doing. "Reiki," came the reply. She told me as much as she could and I was fascinated. A week later a friend called. There was one place left on a Reiki course in Findhorn: would I like to have it? I thought about it and agreed to let her know within a day or two. The following morning I received two letters in the post. The first contained background information about Reiki, and to this day I don't know who sent it. The second was from the woman I had met on the bus. How much more convincing did I need?

Introduction to Reiki

When I met June Woods, my Reiki master, I was struck by her gentleness and by the warmth of her touch. As she introduced me to Reiki, I knew that I had found what had been missing. There were no fireworks and flashing lights—simply a profound sense of coming home. Everything she taught me seemed deeply familiar and felt right. I remember lying in bed with my hands on my heart, energy pouring into me. I knew that I had received more than a healing system. I had a connection to spirit that would become the mainstay of my life.

I returned to London and practiced on everyone I knew. I felt a real sense of purpose growing within me and tried to channel this energy into my work as a photographer. My images changed, I noticed: they became cleaner and simpler than before. But try as I might, I found it hard to integrate my new-found spiritual life with my professional one. I struggled on in London, but it seemed that every unit of effort was reaping fewer rewards than before. Eventually I found myself so broke that it seemed a decision was being forced on me.

At the back of my mind I knew I wanted to take the Reiki master level. I discussed it with my master and resolved to spend a week in retreat meditating on the decision. During one of these meditations I had a vision of a tall man who looked a bit like Merlin wearing a hat and a long coat. He smiled as he approached. I asked him what I should do, at which he laughed and said: "You know very well what you should do. The question is: Do you have the courage?" With that he was gone.

Later that month I received the master initiation from June Woods. It is hard to describe the sensation of energy that filled me, seeming to expand my being beyond anything I could have imagined. It was as if June had stepped inside me and a queue of people behind her did the same. I remember floating about for a few days in a state of complete bliss. Within three weeks of my initiation I had closed my business in London, sold most of my belongings, rented out my flat, and gone to live in a two-man tent in rainy Scotland. I am sure most of my friends and family had decided that I had lost touch with reality. But the exact opposite was true: I was never more in touch. I found my solace in a pack of angel cards. Time after time I picked the same cards: Trust, Faith, and Courage.

The Power of Reiki

Many years later I look back at that time with great fondness. The death and transformation of one's former beliefs and identity is never easy. The Tibetans talk of impermanence, of approaching each moment as if it is your last. The profound connection I had discovered to spirit through Reiki motivated me to surrender to the flow of my life. When I needed support the energy enveloped me with love.

Today I try to travel light; I become uneasy when my belongings get to be more than I can carry. I teach all around the world, but mainly in London and Italy. I never cease to be amazed at the power of Reiki as a transformational healing tool. I continue to grow and learn from those I teach, and Reiki is the power that supports that growth.

I hope that you will find this book a useful reference point at whatever stage you might have reached in your discovery of the world of energy. In drawing from my personal experience of working with Reiki, I present my ideas as guidelines that have been successful for me. I hope they encourage you to find your own way toward truth and help you in your healing.

Chapter 1
What is Reiki?

> *"It is better to light a single candle than curse the darkness."*
>
> CHINESE PROVERB

What is Reiki?

Setting out the basic principles of Reiki: what it is, how it began, and what it can do.

The Chakra System

The ancient theory of the body's seven chakras and our physical, emotional, and psychological relationships with them.

Energetic Bodies: Etheric, Emotional, and Mental

The three further layers of energy around the body: what are their functions and how can we keep them healthy?

How is Dysfunction Caused?

The journey of life: passing through the stages of the seven chakras. How childhood events can resurface as dysfunction later in life, and how to overcome this using Reiki.

Defining Qualities of Reiki

Reiki is a system of healing that originated in Japan and dates back to the end of the nineteenth century. It is practiced by the simple process of the laying on of hands to channel healing energy through the practitioner to the recipient. This healing can take place on many levels.

Above: The Japanese script shows the symbols for the word "Reiki".

Reiki is

- A system of energy healing using spiritually guided life force energy.
- A useful tool for self-awareness and transformation.
- A noninvasive therapy.
- Practiced throughout the world.
- A continuation of teachings given by Reiki grand master Dr. Usui at the end of the nineteenth century.
- An honoring of the Dr. Usui lineage.
- Used in hospitals, private practice, self-care, and in conjunction with many other therapies.

Practiced by transmitting healing energy through the hands.

- Passed on through the initiation process from master to student.
- Healing energy that is guided spiritually.

Reiki is not

- Affiliated with any one religion or religious practice.
- Based on belief, faith, or suggestion.

Rei: The Whole of Creation

Reiki is a Japanese word that translates as "God Light Energy." The easiest way to understand its true meaning is to split the word in two. Rei is directly translated as God or light. It is used to describe the whole of creation—every cell, blade of grass, stone, tree, animal, human, every planet and star. It goes further to describe the creative mind of God. An accurate interpretation of the word Rei could be "All That Is," both in thought and form.

Ki: Life Energy

Ki is the name given to the vital energy that is used to animate and give life to this creation. Just as a model car requires batteries to make it move, so the complex creation of the universe requires a form of energy to animate it. This energy, also known as chi or prana, can be viewed as an ocean that surrounds the physical universe. It provides us with the vitality we require to maintain our health, balance, and well-being on all levels—physical, emotional, mental, and spiritual.

Ki can normally be seen with the naked eye, and appears as dancing electrons of light that move rapidly around. There is an abundance of this energy in nature, and it is most clearly visible in mountainous areas, at the ocean's edge, or in dense forests. Most forms of martial arts, in particular Ki Gong and Tai Chi, acknowledge the presence of this energy and focus on redistributing ki throughout the body to increase health, balance, and well-being.

Above: Ki energy provides us with vitality and well-being.

"*One fish says to another: 'Do you believe in this ocean they talk about?'*"

CHINESE PROVERB

13

What Can Reiki Teach Us?

Reiki is a system of healing that has been developed to bring us directly into contact with the creative intelligence and the vital energy of the universe. This is achieved through a series of transmissions from a Reiki teacher, designed to re-connect us to this universal ki. It is then practiced by developing our awareness of our own energetic self and bringing ki into ourselves to revitalize our body and free it from emotional issues, belief systems, and physical disorders that no longer serve us. As our ability increases and our awareness grows we can allow this energy to flow through us for the benefit of others.

Reiki teaches us that pain, suffering, and illness are caused by separation from the oneness of creation. In other words, it is our loneliness, our feelings of isolation, that cause the pain and suffering. We are on a planet spinning around a solar system and we don't really know where we are going. To most people this is such a frightening realization that it is far easier to completely block it out and focus their attention on something less immediate.

Re-connecting with Ourselves

Deep down, however, it has its effect. If we are honest, most of us have asked ourselves: "What did I do to deserve this? What am I doing here? How did I end up on this planet, surrounded by complete strangers?" The fact is that everyone is feeling the same, and this knowledge is the first step in realizing that we all have something in common. We are all lonely, and the more we strain our eyes looking through telescopes in the hope of finding someone else, the more this only serves to increase this feeling of isolation. We are looking outwardly for something that isn't there. We are looking in the wrong direction.

Reiki is a way of bringing us back home, of re-connecting with the essence of who we are. Reiki is a way to remove the veil that prevents us from experiencing the union with the divine. As we begin to wake up to this idea and walk its path the veil becomes thinner and thinner. We begin to see that it was our fears and beliefs in limitation that created the veil in the first place. So Reiki is a doorway that can re-connect us to the very place we came from. Reiki is a doorway home.

Opposite page: Reiki re-connects you to who you are where you have come from and how you got here.

The Chakra System

I have talked about the ocean of energy that we operate within, and how it can support us energetically. However, for this to happen a mechanism known as the chakra system is required.

Above: The seven chakra centers in the body take the form of funnels that radiate out from the spinal column.

The chakras are centers throughout the body which act like lungs, breathing vital energy from the ocean of energy into our system and distributing it throughout the body along channels known as nadis. Chakra is Sanskrit for wheel, and this serves to describe the spinning motion that the chakras employ to draw this energy into the center of our being.

The Physical Relationship

There are seven main chakra centers throughout the body, each one having a direct relationship to the part of the physical body it governs. The corresponding system on the physical body is called the endocrine system.

The chakra system is made up of a single vertical power channel, running from the top of the head (the crown center) down the spine, to the coccyx (the base center). These two chakras at each end of the spine open out like funnels from the narrow vertical channel. This vertical power current forms our connection to spirit and earth. Along this vertical current are five chakras, forming horizontal intersections evenly distributed along its length. Each of these appears as a pair, with one facing the front and the other facing the back. Viewed from the side these look like open-ended funnels, radiating out from the spinal column.

16

How the Chakras Look

The seven chakras, each of which possesses its own color and relates to a different part of the body, are evenly arranged around the physical spinal column.

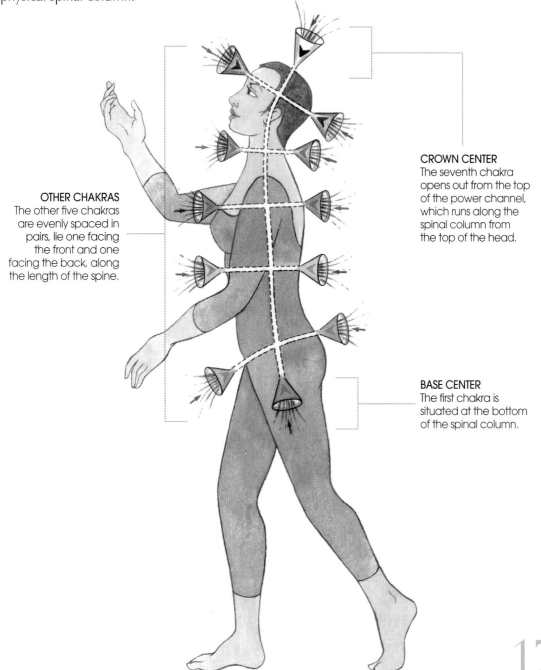

CROWN CENTER
The seventh chakra opens out from the top of the power channel, which runs along the spinal column from the top of the head.

OTHER CHAKRAS
The other five chakras are evenly spaced in pairs, lie one facing the front and one facing the back, along the length of the spine.

BASE CENTER
The first chakra is situated at the bottom of the spinal column.

The Emotional and Psychological Relationship

In addition to the chakras' relationship with the physical body, each also has a relationship with our emotional and psychological selves. We develop each chakra for a period of seven years, before moving on to the next one. This begins at birth, as we emerge from the protection of our mother's womb and start to develop our relationship with the outside world. The chakras represent a journey beginning at the base, or first chakra, and moving up through each chakra in turn every seven years, until at the age of forty-nine we arrive at the crown. At the end of our forty-ninth year the cycle is complete and we return again to the first chakra.

In this way, the chakras can be seen as a logical progression through life as we learn to deal with the outside world and its relationship with our own inner world. The soul incarnates in the physical world, which is represented by the vertical line from spirit to Earth. Then the soul goes through five levels of interaction with the world as it develops its physical, emotional, psychological, and spiritual self.

Below: Our emotional development throughout our lives corresponds to our cycle through the seven chakras, each one lasting seven years from birth to the age of forty nine. The heart is the central chakra, through which the universal love radiates.

The Seven Main Chakras and their Related Aspects

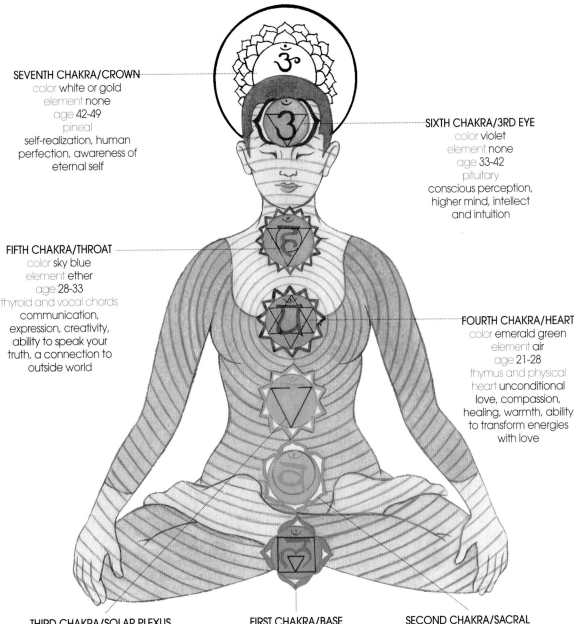

SEVENTH CHAKRA/CROWN
color white or gold
element none
age 42-49
pineal
self-realization, human
perfection, awareness of
eternal self

SIXTH CHAKRA/3RD EYE
color violet
element none
age 33-42
pituitary
conscious perception,
higher mind, intellect
and intuition

FIFTH CHAKRA/THROAT
color sky blue
element ether
age 28-33
thyroid and vocal chords
communication,
expression, creativity,
ability to speak your
truth, a connection to
outside world

FOURTH CHAKRA/HEART
color emerald green
element air
age 21-28
thymus and physical
heart unconditional
love, compassion,
healing, warmth, ability
to transform energies
with love

THIRD CHAKRA/SOLAR PLEXUS
color yellow
element fire
age 14-21
spleen, liver, gall bladder, and
pancreas
power, control, identity,
empathy, relationships, activity,
ability to accept others

FIRST CHAKRA/BASE
color red
element earth
age 1-7
kidneys/adrenals
security, foundations of
life, trust in life, ability to
manifest what you need

SECOND CHAKRA/SACRAL
color orange
element water
age 7-14
sexual organs, and bladder,
emotions, self-worth, sexuality,
open expression, being able to
give and receive

The Energetic Body

As well as the physical layer around the human body, there are believed to be seven further layers, which increase in vibration the further from the physical body they are. These layers are referred to as the energetic bodies.

For the purpose of our work I will simplify these down to three layers.
• The etheric body
• The emotional body
• The mental body

The Etheric Body

The first of these bodies is known as the etheric body. This is visible to most people as an aura around the physical body of a person, extending out to approximately 2 in (5 cm). It appears to the naked eye as a moving light, almost flame-like, and constantly in motion.

The etheric body draws vital energy from the ocean of energy through the solar plexus chakra and distributes this energy, via the chakra system and nadis, into the physical body. When the body is receiving healthy amounts of vital energy this will be reflected in the strength of the etheric field around it. This etheric body can be photographed using a technique known as Kirlian photography. The etheric field is made up of rays of light that radiate out from the physical. The stronger the rays emitted the more vitality is contained in the physical. These rays of light make up a protective web of light around the physical and appear to be magnetically charged and polarized. In a healthy state they appear straight, but when disrupted can become tangled or bent.

Nurturing Your Etheric Body

Our interaction with nature is an important part of nurturing our etheric bodies, as trees, flowers and plants have similar etheric bodies to our own and can be used to recharge our energy. You may find sitting with your back to a tree or smelling and breathing in the scents of flowers to be of great benefit. Conversely, spending time around electrical appliances such as computers, mobile telephones, and televisions can have a negative effect on you as they scramble the electromagnetic field of energy around you. This is due to the high levels of electromagnetic radiation emitted by such devices. If you must be around these devices then regular breaks are important. In addition, unhealthy lifestyles including the abuse of drugs or alcohol can also have a detrimental effect on the strength of this body. One of the most powerful healing aspects of Reiki is in maintaining high levels of vitality within this etheric body. This will serve to protect you from illness and disruptive electromagnetic radiation whenever it enters your field of energy. It will also be of great benefit in helping you clear such external invasions from your field. We will talk about how this is possible in the chapter on First Degree Reiki.

Energy on film

Kirlian photography is a unique system that enables us to record the etheric energy field on film. The photographs are, in effect, negative images where light is represented by black and vice versa. It is of great benefit to be able to show the effects of Reiki on the energy field, as the examples below show.

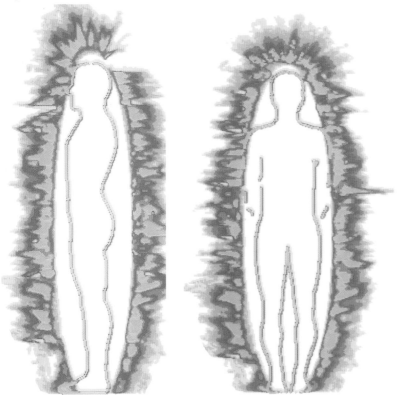

Left: The perfect etheric body
These images show the etheric, emotional, and mental energy fields of a balanced and healthy person. The etheric field is closest to the physical body.

Relationships

The dynamic of "like attracts like" is played out most often in our personal relationships. When we feel a very strong attraction to a person we are literally pulled together by an energy interaction taking place in our emotional fields. We experience this as falling in love. We move on to the bliss of union, for what is commonly called the honeymoon period. Then things start to change: issues start to surface as our partner reflects back to us our deepest, unconscious fears about relationships. Trust, ownership, betrayal, freedom, anger, and fear can begin to surface.

The Emotional Body

The second layer of the energetic body is known as the emotional body, which reflects the emotional state of the person. Those people who have developed their ability to see energy fields report this body as being made up of colors that are constantly changing, and radiate out from the physical body from 1½–5 ft (0.5–1 m), depending on the person being viewed. These colors change depending on the emotions being experienced. Emotions such as anger and fear will appear as dark clouds, whereas love and joy will appear as bright, glowing colors.

The Emotional Signature

In addition to immediate feelings and emotions, the emotional body holds all the unresolved emotional conflicts and fears relating back to a person's early life. These fears and conflicts are transmitted to the external world, via the chakras, as an unconscious message. We refer to this as the emotional signature of a person, and the simple rule of "like attracts like" reflects this message. The signature we send out into the world will act like a magnet, drawing us to situations and experiences that reflect our unconscious fears and emotions. In this way, the world can be seen as a mirror in which to observe our own unconscious selves.

If somebody is unconsciously angry then the people or situations they attract will reflect that anger. They might consider themselves to be loving and peaceful, while unconsciously sending out deeply aggressive energy signals. The signals they send out will draw experiences to them that reflect this aggression. The purpose of this mirroring is to bring our unresolved issues up onto the conscious level. Once we are aware of the signals we are sending out into the world, and understand the law of attraction, we can begin to take responsibility and start to change them.

Reiki plays an important part in this process. When we receive Reiki it gives us high vibrational energy, which works to stimulate low vibrational clouds in our emotional body and make them vibrate at higher and higher rates. As they vibrate higher, the memory of the experience that caused the clouds to be formed is released, allowing us to re-experience it and forgive ourselves and the people involved. The memory held in the emotional body, and its effect on the physical body, is then released, and we can unfurl like a closed leaf, reaching full growth as emotionally healthy beings.

Radiating Energy

The energy field of the emotional body is made up of colors that constantly change according to the emotions being experienced. Feelings of joy, fear, and conflict are transmitted by the seven chakras.

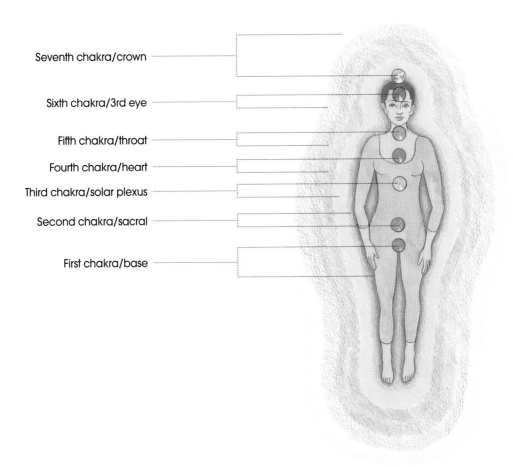

Seventh chakra/crown

Sixth chakra/3rd eye

Fifth chakra/throat

Fourth chakra/heart

Third chakra/solar plexus

Second chakra/sacral

First chakra/base

23

The Mental Body

The third layer of the energetic body is known as the mental body, which radiates out to around 9 ft (3 m) around the physical body. This field of energy holds our beliefs about reality, formed throughout our lives. Belief systems reflect the culture we have been brought up in, the beliefs we have inherited from our parents, our religion, and our peer groups. The mental body reflects our rational mind and perceptions on a physical level. The experiences we have in the physical body are processed in the mental body after having passed through the emotional body. Therefore, our perceptions and rational thoughts are often deeply affected by any unresolved issues on the emotional level.

This field of energy is very much like a transmitter and receiver. We pick up on the thought projections of the people around us, and the unconscious messages being sent into the world through sources such as television and newspapers. These projections are often fearful and concerned with worldly matters. We absorb these and hold them in our own energy field—we start to believe they belong to us. Our own perception of the world can then become clouded by this invasion of negative thought patterns, and we will find our attention becomes focused on these issues.

What we think is what we become. When we send our beliefs about ourselves out into the world, they are reflected back to confirm our thoughts. So if we believe the world is a dark place, and that we are powerless victims of it, the world will oblige us by reflecting our beliefs and presenting us with situations and people that support these beliefs.

The true function of the mental body is to marry the conscious mind with intuitive perception. Once we are aware of our access to the mind of God we are able to respond to the information and signals we receive on an intuitive level and translate them into a more solid form. So, as our chakra system suggests, we are a bridge between spirit and earth, and part of our function is to access the information given by spirit and utilize it here on earth.

Ripples in a Pond

In meditation, I was shown how thoughts are like ripples in a still pond. Once formed they are sent out in all directions. I was invited to play with different thoughts—positive and negative—to show me their different qualities. I was shocked and amazed at how real they were. It was as if I could touch them.

The cleansing of the emotional body of its unresolved issues is vital for this process to take place without distortion. While we may receive clear and precise guidance, our own issues can distort this information or manipulate it to serve our own needs. Our beliefs can also block this perception, as it may threaten our limited view of reality.

Layers of Energy

The body's energy fields are in three layers: the etheric body, which contains vital energy; the emotional body, which holds unresolved emotional conflicts; and the mental body, which reflects our rational mind and perceptions.

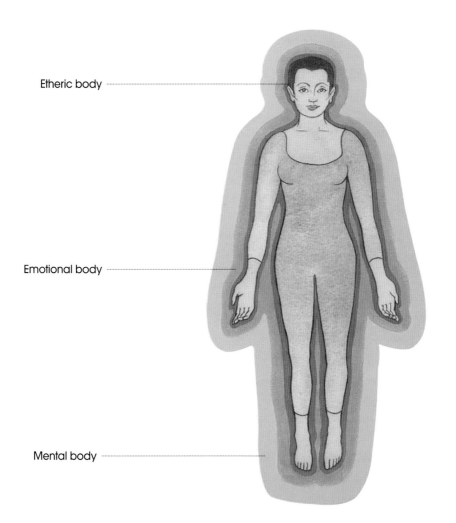

Etheric body

Emotional body

Mental body

How is Dysfunction Caused?

As the description of the chakras and the energetic bodies demonstrates, our lives are a journey, and during this journey we develop ourselves on all levels. The outside world and the people around us play an important role in the shaping of who we are, both emotionally and in terms of our beliefs about the world.

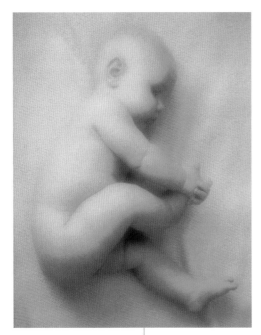

Above: As babies, we develop our base chakra, which is concerned with the kidneys and adrenals. Our issues of security and trust are addressed.

As we grow up, we develop emotional patterns that are based on those of the people around us. We also inherit the belief systems of our immediate environment, so in a sense we begin to mimic the behaviour of others as a way of validating our own beliefs. We learn how to function in the world through the teachings and guidance we receive from those around us.

Case Study

From birth to the age of seven, our subject is developing her base chakra, and if her basic needs are not met by her parents, she will begin to lose trust in her ability to survive. At the age of eight she moves into the next stage of her development, her second chakra, and is working on issues such as sexuality, self-worth, feelings, and emotions. She is looking to expand her horizons, she wants to fit in with her peer group, and her self-worth depends on it.

At the age of nine our child's parents move home. Suddenly she is ripped away from the surroundings that are familiar to her. She has already developed issues relating to security and trust, and now they are enforced with a new set of issues.

At the age of fifteen our subject moves into her third chakra. She is working with issues of control, power, and her personal identity. She is, however, very fragile, as she carries unconscious fears that the world is a dangerous place, and is still very dependent on her parents.

At the age of twenty one
Our subject moves into her heart center, the fourth chakra, at 21 developing issues related to love. She meets someone and falls in love. She wants so much to love and be loved but for some reason it doesn't work out that way. Issues from her earlier life are starting to surface and they are preventing her from having the relationship she wants. Unexpressed anger, insecurity, and the need for control start to surface.

Our subject moves into her fifth chakra, the throat, at the age of twenty eight. Now she is dealing with all forms of expression and communication and is at the age where all she has learned is beginning to take form. However, her feelings of insecurity are preventing her from expressing herself fully in all areas of life.

Below: During life, we pass through a cycle of seven chakras, ending at age forty nine. We then begin with a new cycle, starting again at the base chakra.

At the age of thirty five
She moves into the sixth chakra at thirty five years old. She is developing her own conscious perception of herself. If, by this stage in her life, she has failed to look at some of her own deep-seated fears and unresolved issues they may surface more strongly.

At the age of forty two
At forty two she moves into her last cycle, the seventh chakra, and begins to develop understanding of her eternal self. She may yearn to travel to lonely places, embarking on voyages of discovery to find

Opposite page:

Emotional issues can effect any chakra and are carried with you as you proceed through life.

herself. If she does not allow this flowering to occur she will remain in the conflicting cycle of her previous forty two years.

We pass through each stage of development as the relevant issues relating to that chakra are worked on. After the forty ninth year we will return again to start a new cycle starting with the base chakra.

Lightening the Load

Quite often we can ignore and suppress thoughts, feelings, and unresolved issues, choosing to find ways to cope in spite of them. However, this is like carrying excess baggage that simply weighs us down, serving no purpose other than to limit us. If we can identify this excess baggage we may find it is no longer needed—we can continue on our journey with a lighter load.

It is impossible to separate our emotions from our physical body—they are all connected. If we carry unresolved issues on an emotional level, the chakra that was being developed at the time the issue occurred will be affected too. This may mean the flow of vital energy reaching the physical body served by that chakra will be affected as well. Consequently, we find that issues related to any chakra will have an effect on each layer of the three bodies related to it.

Chapter 2
Raising Self-Awareness

"Native Americans say life is like walking backwards: it is easy to see where you have been, not so easy to see where you are going."

Introduction
Developing self-awareness is the first step toward understanding how to avoid the pitfalls of life.

Exercises
Connection to the Earth and Spirit
How to experience the rhythms of the earth, sun, and moon.

Internal Scanning
Relieving pain throughout the body by visualization.

Etheric Gazing
How focused observation can reveal hidden depths.

Our Friends and Family as a Mirror
Study your true feelings toward friends and family.

Inner Child
Drawing on the wisdom of the inner child to resolve everyday problems.

Understanding the Male/ Female Split
A clear demonstration of the male and female principles that we carry.

The Importance of Touch
Sometimes a gentle touch, a helping hand, or a hug, is the best medicine.

Raising Self-Awareness

When we look back on our lives it is easy to see where we have made mistakes, and what we would do differently with hindsight. This is part of the learning process: through the trials and tribulations of life we grow and evolve.

This gradual evolution raises our personal awareness so that we can recognize possible pitfalls ahead.

This works very well as long as we remember what has taken place in the past. However, much of our memory has been suppressed and is stored on a cellular or unconscious level. It resides in our energetic fields, affecting us and our daily lives although we can't see how. It is important to start to examine ourselves to find out how we create the pitfalls of our life unconsciously. What unconscious behavior, beliefs, and unresolved emotional issues do we carry around that shape and influence us?

The following pages contain exercises which can help you to develop self-awareness. These exercises ask some of the following questions.

- Where am I?
- What is going on inside me?
- What am I carrying with me?
- What does the outside world mirror for me?
- How have I changed?

Above and opposite: The diversity of life around you and awareness of your surroundings is important in understanding the nature of Reiki.

Exercise 1

Connection to the Earth and Spirit

Find an open space in nature to do this exercise:

- To begin, stand with your feet parallel and shoulder-width apart. Leave your arms loose beside you and bend your knees a little. Begin to take deep breaths, inhaling through your nose down into your belly, and exhaling through your mouth. Take time to find your natural rhythm—do not force the breath.

- As you breathe become aware of the ground beneath you. What does your connection with the earth feel like? Do you feel grounded, or are you floating above the earth? Imagine the full globe of the earth below you. You are standing on it as it slowly rotates in space. It is your means of survival—your ship as you travel through space. See the image of yourself on the globe. See the beauty of the earth below you.

- Now imagine the sun above you. As you continue to breathe, draw the energy from the sun into your body, through the top of your head, down into your belly. As you breathe out, imagine the energy traveling down through your base and your feet into the earth like the roots of a tree. Keep breathing in your natural rhythm. Feel yourself supported and grounded on the earth and connected to the sun. Feel the warmth of the sun as it bathes you in its nourishing light. Feel the natural balance between the earth, yourself, and the sun.

- Now imagine the moon below the earth, its silent rhythms pulling the seas of the earth downward. Feel this pull within yourself. Imagine yourself on the earth, the sun above bathing you in light, the moon below pulling you downward gently. Experience being a part of the natural rhythms of the earth, the moon, and the sun. Inhale, exhale, and simply feel.

Left: Imagine yourself standing on top of the earth, and mentally affirm your strong connection with it.

35

Exercise 2

Opposite:

Internal scanning allows you to journey around your body, pinpointing any areas suffering pain and becoming aware of emotions that may be associated with that discomfort.

Internal Scanning

For this exercise you will need to draw on your powers of visualization and concentration.

• To begin, find a safe place where you will not be disturbed. Lie on your back or sit in the lotus position. Make sure you are comfortable and warm.

• Close your eyes, take a few deep breaths, and relax.

• Now focus your awareness inside yourself. Start at your feet and work your way up your body slowly. Ask yourself what you feel. Are you relaxed? What does your body feel like? As you move through your body you may find areas of discomfort. Don't try to make yourself more comfortable by moving around. Instead give the discomfort your full attention and find out what it is made of. Any pain in the body will contain emotions too. Become aware of the feelings contained within the pain. Allow the pain to be, and if it moves somewhere else follow it. Try to relax into the pain.

• Continue on through your body. When you find other painful areas focus on them and again see what emotions they contain. Journey through your whole body in this way.

Exercise 3

Opposite: Find a quiet, calm setting where you will not be disturbed, and ensure that your partner is willing to devote themselves entirely to the exercise.

Etheric Gazing

This exercise involves a friend or partner. Before beginning the exercise be sure that you are both willing and committed to engage deeply with each other.

• Sit close together, facing each other either in a chair or on the floor. Try to ensure that you are both sitting in front of a plain wall, as this is less distracting.

• Hold your partner's hands and begin to look into each other's eyes. Question how it feels to be watched and seen. Examine which side of the face you feel more connected to. Which side are you drawn to look at? Allow yourself to connect deeply with the person and examine what they are holding in their face. Are they in pain, and if so where? Is it evident more on one side than the other?

• If you find that the face changes shape, continue with the exercise and observe what changes take place. There may be a darkening of the features, a little like someone turning the lights down, which indicates that you are seeing the person on an etheric level. The features may also change radically: you may see male features on a female face; younger or older faces; or even animal features. Continue with the exercise for about ten minutes and then gently disconnect. Spend time sharing what you saw in each other—you will be surprised at what you have within you.

This exercise can also be done on your own using a mirror. It is a little harder to remain objective but can still be of great benefit.

Exercise 4

Opposite:
Try to record your reactions to your family and friends, allowing yourself to experience your emotions, and noting which areas of your body react to their presence.

Our Friends and Family as a Mirror

Spend time with your friends and family and really listen to what they say about themselves and how they think about the world.

• What goes on inside yourself as you interact with these people? Remember that your family and friends are mirrors for you.

• Instead of reacting to the feelings you are experiencing, try to observe them. Write your feelings down. Place your hands on the areas of your body that are affected and allow yourself to experience all your feelings.

  • Is your body supportive?
  • Does your body empower them?
  • How do you feel when you are with your family and friends?
  • Which areas of your body react to them?
  • Does your solar plexus contract?
  • Do you get a stomach ache?
  • Does your throat hurt?
  • Do you feel angry, scared, nervous, unable to think?

Exercise 5

Opposite: Use old photographs of yourself as a child to discover long-forgotten emotions.

Inner Child

For this exercise you need to look through the family album. Find a photograph of yourself as a child that you are in some way attracted to: maybe you like the way you are dressed, or the confidence you exuded. Place it where it can be seen on a regular basis throughout the day. Carry it with you to and from work. Say good morning and good night to the child in the photograph. Begin to build a relationship with the child. Look at who you were.

- Ask the child: "Have I turned out OK? What should I change?" Draw on the wisdom of the child within to teach and guide you. If you are in a situation that makes you unhappy, ask your child what they would do to remedy matters.

- What do you feel when you look at this photograph?
- What qualities do you resonate with when you look at the child?
- What can you learn from this child?
- What does this child need?
- What were his/her dreams? Remember that this child is still within you.
- Did you fulfill those dreams?

As an individual with a conscious awareness of who you are, you can start to develop compassion for others. Recognizing that each person is doing the best they can on their chosen path leads to an acceptance of others, and an understanding of where you stand on your own path.

Understanding the Male/ Female Split

One of the main sources of conflict in the world is between men and women. However, it is often forgotten that we carry both masculine and feminine principles within us, regardless of our physical sex.

The photographs opposite are part of an experiment to demonstrate the male/female split. Each photograph is a composite made up of a single portrait, the original being duplicated in its mirrored reflection. The photographs are split in two and rejoined with the two left sides of the face together, and the two right sides of the face together. In Reiki the left side of the face represents the female, and the right side the male.

The effects are startling, showing widely different features, expressions, and shapes in the two faces. The two sides reveal the emotional conflicts that are held in the physical features themselves. The imbalance of power between the masculine and feminine within each person is also highlighted.

"All pain, all suffering, is caused by separateness."

BARBARA ANN BRENNAN

Masculine and Feminine Sides

Regardless of our gender, the left side of the face represents the female principle of our personality, and the right side, the male. These images, made by duplicating one side of the face in its mirrored reflection, show how the male and female sides of the same person can show completely different characteristics.

Original photograph

Right side—masculine principle

Left side—feminine principle

The Importance of Touch

Our ability to touch one another gives us extraordinary healing strength and this, combined with the healing power of Reiki, can take our abilities to new levels. Using our instinctive knowledge, we can use our hands to do good things – to bring well-being, health and happiness to all those who need it.

Opposite: Our hands are our sacred healing tools. Touch allows us to comfort and heal with them and the important power of Reiki lets us take that healing deeper and deeper.

When we hurt ourselves as children it is an instinctive action to put our hand on the painful place and "rub it better". The fact that we are capable of healing forms part of our inner wisdom. Often a person will need nothing more than a gentle touch, a helping hand, or a hug to make them feel better. However, in this hi-tech world of ours it is easy to forget the healing power of touch.

As you learn to embrace Reiki you will find that your natural tendency to rub things better takes on deep significance. I remember a story an elderly lady told me during a flight from Scotland to London. We chatted about my work with Reiki and, to my surprise, she told me that she thought it was the most natural thing in the world. She related that she had been in hospital earlier that year for a small operation and the doctor, realizing she might be a little frightened, had kindly taken her on a tour of the hospital. He had shown her all the life-saving machines that they used in order, I suppose, to instill confidence in her. At the end of the tour, the patient looked at the doctor and said: "Very impressive machines, but where do you do the healing?" He didn't understand what she meant. "Where do you use your hands?" she asked, "Where do you give healing?" The doctor replied that they didn't do that in the hospital. The lady was surprised and said, `But doctor, you can't heal without touch."

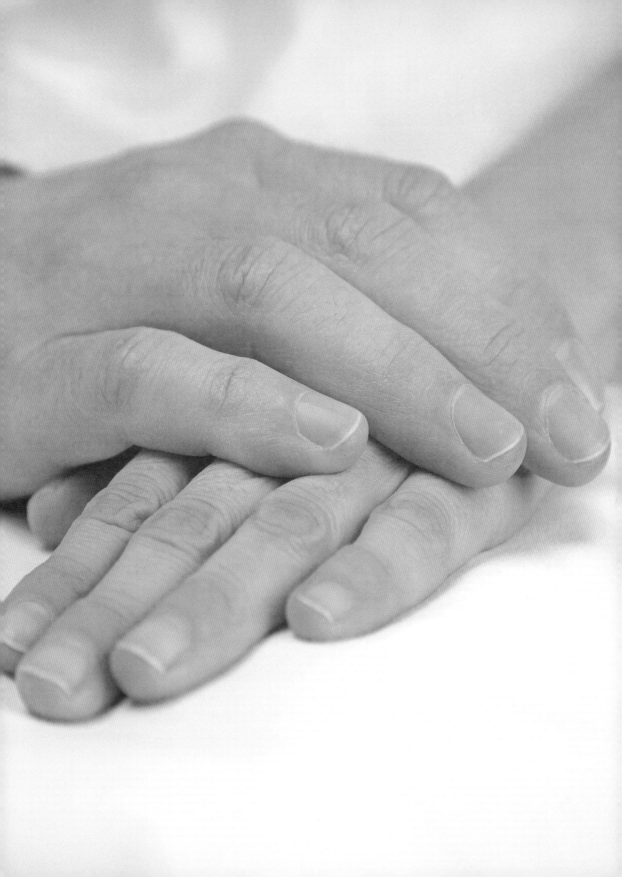

Chapter 3
First Degree Reiki

"*I found myself standing at the edge of a cliff looking into an abyss. I knew I had to jump but I was afraid. A hand took mine and a voice gently said 'We can do this together if it will be easier for you'.*"

First Degree Reiki
An introduction to this fundamental level of Reiki teaching.

How Classes are Structured
What to expect when you attend a Reiki course: group sharing and first treatments.

Initiations
To start practicing Reiki, you need to be initiated by a master. This is a simple but intense process.

Foundation Treatment and Invocation
Outlines the preparation the Reiki practitioner must carry out before beginning a session.

Full Body Treatment
Full step-by-step instructions for performing a full Reiki treatment, showing how to heal specific problems.

Short Treatment
If you are faced with time restrictions, here are ways to experience the benefits of Reiki without giving a full treatment.

Self-Treatment
Treat yourself to keep your connection with the Reiki energy clear and open.

First Degree Reiki

When Dr. Usui first received the Reiki vision and empowerment on the top of Mount Kurama it was an enormously powerful experience. The energy was so strong that it rendered him unconscious.

Above: First Degree Reiki is an introspective journey into the self, away from the crowd.

A t the time, Dr. Usui chose to accept the levels of energy that he received. He later decided that, in order for Reiki to be passed on in a safe and responsible way, he would need to develop his teaching in stages. These different levels would be supported with an initiation, or series of initiations, which would facilitate a change in the person's energy field. The idea was that while this initiation would be strong enough to facilitate a transformation it would not knock the student out.

Today we teach Reiki in this way, with three main levels, each having a specific set of teachings designed to help the student expand in awareness and develop understanding of energy work at a sensible pace. In today's world of instant gratification, Reiki maintains its tried and tested methods of slowly traveling the path to self-discovery on an energetic level. We are all unique and the journey will be different for everyone.

What is First Degree Reiki?

The first level of Reiki is primarily for the self. It is an experiential journey into awareness of the world of energy, both internal and external. The objective is to discover ways in which the student can clear their personal vessel and become a distinct and open channel for the universal life force energy to flow through them.

This journey begins by being opened to the flow of this energy through the initiation process. After the initiation the student must learn to work with the new energy that flows through them. This involves learning to let go of the limitations our minds impose on us and embrace a new world of possibilities. Students are made aware of their own energy, discovering ways in which they can observe themselves objectively. They are given the opportunity to discover a part of themselves that has remained hidden or asleep.

First degree Reiki is an opportunity to access the obstacles that prevent people from living in harmony. These blocks may exist emotionally, mentally, or physically, but within the safe and supportive workshop environment we can begin to understand and resolve those inner conflicts. This takes courage: students are asked to face parts of themselves that they have not acknowledged for many years.

The first level is also the introduction to working with energy in a practical way. Students are given set treatments that lay the foundation for future work with energy. They learn how to listen, with their whole body, and establish a connection with their own intuition.

Building Trust

The relationship with the teacher is important in helping the student to establish the right time to move on to the next level. It is generally agreed that three months should elapse between first and second degree Reiki, and that a period of a year should be allowed before moving on to the third level.

Left: Before completing a Reiki course, you will need to undergo an initiation process, forming bonds with your Reiki teacher.

51

How Classes are Structured

Reiki is taught verbally, with very little need to take notes or study. The basic principles behind the teachings are simple, and are explained in an informal way.

Anatomy of a Reiki Course

Each master will structure his or her class to suit their teaching methods. However, all first degree courses should include:

- A verbal introduction giving the history of Reiki methods and practices.
- A description of the subtle anatomy of a human being and its effect on our lives.
- Initiations (traditionally there are four, although some masters may give two or even just one).
- A description and demonstration of full/foundation treatment with practice.
- The self treatment.
- The short treatment.
- Information on how to treat animals, plants, and your environment.
- What to do in emergencies.
- And, importantly, lots of hugs.

The history of Reiki is recounted, telling us how this system of healing was discovered, and how it came to be in its present form. The classes are usually held over two days.

The first morning is dedicated to group bonding and self-awareness exercises. These exercises make the students aware of how they are feeling, and teach them to concentrate their attention on their internal self through guided meditations. Group sharing gives people the opportunity to tell each other about their own personal journey and what brought them to this point in their lives. It is often encouraging to hear similar stories to your own, as it helps to validate your experiences as being real. All these exercises are an important part of the process of helping people to relax and feel less inhibited.

After the first morning the work becomes experiential and is centered around the initiations. These are powerful exchanges of energy from the master to the student, and often the students will require time to sleep as they integrate the experience. Time is put aside for any questions that may need to be asked, or any processing that needs to take place.

The first afternoon is devoted to receiving and giving treatments for the first time. It is often a period of astonishment, as each student becomes aware of their capacity to channel energy. They spend time growing accustomed to the strange new sensations passing through their hands and bodies, as they learn to recognize what different energies feel like.

The second day is dedicated to teaching the self treatment, the short treatment, and discussing ways in which Reiki can be used on a daily basis to enhance your life. The positions of the full treatment are covered and time is given to allow any personal transformations within the group to take place.

Below: Early on in a Reiki course, the students will participate in group discussions and sharing, telling each other about their own personal journeys.

Initiations

There are four initiations in the first degree Reiki course, based on the original teachings of Dr. Usui. They are designed to open up our ability to channel the healing energy of the universe more effectively.

Above: Like a burning candle, the Reiki that rushes into a student after initiation can take the form of heat and energy.

Every person is connected, whether they are conscious of it or not, to the universal energy. This connection is enhanced through the Reiki initiation process. In addition, it is a guarantee of the lineage or pathway that the energy follows before flowing through you. It forms the foundation of our connection to this energy and the specific spiritual guidance that accompanies it.

Though deeply profound and moving, the process of initiation is very simple. The master acts as a channel through which the guides and energy work. The guides of the person receiving the initiation are also present. The master follows a series of movements, placing symbols into key energy points in the student. These serve to anchor the Reiki vibration into their physical, mental, emotional, and spiritual bodies.

The master begins with the crown center then, in a flowing sequence, will work through the third eye, the heart, and the root centers to anchor the energy. The master will then continue

"We are all like pendulums: Start a bunch of pendulums swinging randomly and come back a while later to find that they are all swinging in resonance. Given a little help and encouragement, we will all move toward resonance with each other."

DANAAN PARRY

through the hand chakras, to allow the healing energy to flow from the heart through the hands. Finally, the student is grounded by connecting the energy to the two chakras in the feet. This initiation is very powerful and, once anchored, remains for life. After the initiation the student will normally feel strong rushes of heat through their main vertical power channel down the spine. Their hands will become very hot as they are charged with the energy.

The initiations are seen as healings in themselves. They introduce such a powerful love vibration into the student's field of energy that any lower vibrational thought patterns and emotions start to rise up into the consciousness. Because of this, a period of integration is required, said to be approximately twenty-one days. This three-week period is often accompanied by a fair amount of turbulence as old feelings, memories, and experiences begin to surface. During this time of transformation it is important to apply the self-healing techniques learnt during the first degree course.

Above: The energy channels are opened through the initiation, a powerful yet simple process that connects us to Reiki.

55

Foundation Treatment

When you commence a Reiki session it is important to come to it fully prepared. Take the time to attend to your personal preparation before you start thinking about giving Reiki to another.

Above: Relaxation
At the beginning of the session, allow the client to close their eyes and relax into it.

Preparation

A session begins before the person arrives and ends after they have left. It is important that you spend some time preparing yourself and the space around you for what you are about to do.

- Burn some incense to clear any stagnant energy that may exist.
- Ensure the room temperature is comfortable.
- Play gentle music to help the client relax.
- Have some fresh drinking water to hand, as energy work tends to dehydrate you and your client.
- Use fresh, clean linen and keep a warm blanket to cover the client if they get cold.
- Put all telephones on silent and make sure you will not be disturbed.

Once everything is ready sit still and focus inward on yourself. Take a few moments to scan through your energy field and take note of how you are feeling. It is important to identify and own the feelings that are yours so that you do not project them onto your client. In an ideal world you will be clear of any personal issues, but this is seldom the case. Use the invocation prayer to invite your guides and helpers into the room with you. Use their energy to give yourself ten minutes of Reiki into the heart center and solar plexus. This will ensure you are fully centered.

First Impressions

It is important to record your first impressions when you meet the client. What is their body language telling you? Perhaps they have their arms crossed tightly over their solar plexus to protect themself. This could mean that they have an issue related to that chakra.

Introduce yourself and, if it is their first time receiving Reiki, explain a little about its background and methods. Chat to them and make them feel relaxed.

Above: Invocation
Invoke your guides and angels and feel the presence of the energy as it surrounds you.

Left: It is improtant to discuss any concerns or queries you may have before commencing with any Reiki treatment.

57

Invocation

Before we start giving a Reiki treatment it is important to go through the correct preparation. One important aspect is to invoke our healing guides in the Reiki lineage, going right back to the Reiki source. This ensures that our healing power comes from the right place.

O ne of the unique aspects of working with Reiki is the connection to the lineage of Dr. Usui. Through the initiation process we have a specific pathway that forms our connection to the Reiki. As we work with the energy we become part of this lineage and can call on that lineage to assist us in our work.

The power of invocation and prayer is an important part of the healing process, helping us to verbally state our intention for the healing we are about to do.

By calling on our guides, the Reiki masters, and the universal energy we are empowering and affirming our intention. This ensures that we are creating a safe environment for ourselves and those who come to us, and that we will be protected at all times. It is also an important part of surrendering to the free flow of energy through us, helping us to remember our connection to the universe, and the origins of the energy we are using.

On the opposite page is a powerful invocation that can be used for this purpose. It can also be repeated as you begin the healing session. Of course, it is not always possible to prepare yourself in this way. If you are working in an emergency or in a public place it is advisable to invoke your helpers silently as you are working.

If you feel a connection to a particular guide, angel, or ascended master you can include them in your invocation.

The Reiki Family

I would describe my experience of invocation as being like having a family that I am connected to through the initiation process. When I call on the energy, the family comes too.

"I am the presence calling on the universal life force energy to come from source through Christ with love, light, and wisdom. I ask for my guides and angels to be with me to guide and protect me. I ask for the Reiki masters past and present to be with me, in particular the grand masters Dr. Usui, Dr. Hayashi, and Hawayo Takata. I ask that they ensure all that takes place is of the very highest good for all concerned. I am the love of God, I am the light of God, I am the healing power of God. I am. I am. I am."

Full Body Treatment

Smoothing the Aura

Before treatment begins, smooth the aura by gently stroking your hands from the head to the feet in a circular motion. This helps to settle the receiver's energy in preparation for the healing session, and also seals the energies in at the end of a session. By gently stroking your hands through the aura, approximately 8 in (20 cm) from the body, you are able to feel any imbalances in the receiver's energy centers. I suggest the use of aurosoma pomanders and quintessence for this technique.

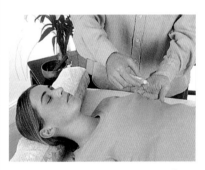

Using Aurosoma to clear the field

Aurosoma is used to smooth the auric field at the beginning and end of treatments.

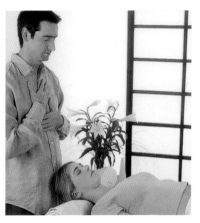

Tuning In

Take a few moments to center yourself and connect with the Reiki energy before entering the patient's energy field.

Smoothing the Aura

Gently stroke your hand through the aura to feel for energy imbalances.

Front Positions

1. Over the Forehead, Eyes, and Cheeks For the treatment of eye problems, sinuses, colds, allergies, nerves in the brain, pituitary and pineal gland. Effective in balancing the pineal gland, which is the center of hormonal regulation. This position helps the client to relax, and stimulates and balances the sixth chakra.

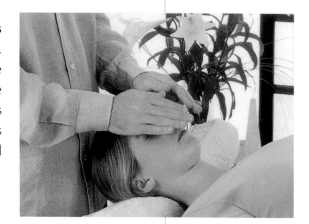

2. To the Sides of the Temples For the treatment of optic nerves, and effective in balancing the right and left sides of the brain. This position is very relaxing for clients suffering from stress.

3. Over the Ears Treats many organs, via the acupuncture points in this area, including the heart, intestines, kidneys, lungs, stomach, liver, and gall bladder.

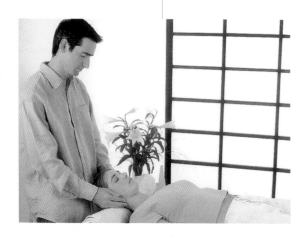

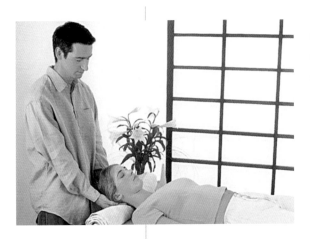

4. Back of the Head Place your fingertips on the medulla oblongata, which is connected to the third eye. This position is good for eyes, vision, headaches, nose bleeds, stroke, and the pineal gland. Memory bank for all childhood and past-life emotional trauma.

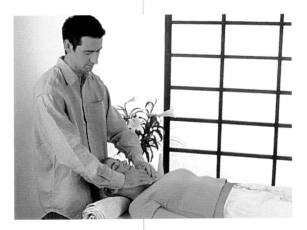

5. Throat Relates to the fifth chakra. For sore throat, flu, high blood pressure, anger, the thyroid gland, frustration, and problems with expression. The throat chakra is deeply connected with communication and creativity.

6. Thymus Gland/Upper Chest This is where we feel fear, panic, stress, and a whole range of emotions. It is known as the survival spot, and affects energy levels. People often feel a sense of suffocation in this area when their heart chakra closes, which reveals problems with relating to others.

7. Solar Plexus and Heart These relate to the third and fourth chakras. Treat the solar plexus for digestive problems and patterns of behavior, and the heart for emotional blockages, circulation, stress, and heart problems. The fourth chakra affects our ability to love ourselves and others on all possible levels.

8. Liver and Spleen For the treatment of toxification on all levels, suppression of anger, bitterness, sadness, and depression. This area also includes the gall bladder and the pancreas.

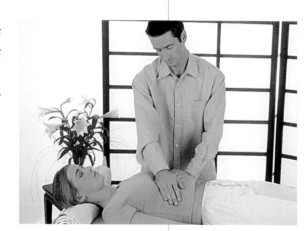

9. Hara/Belly Deals with the suppression of all issues relating to power. This area also includes the intestines and the duodenum.

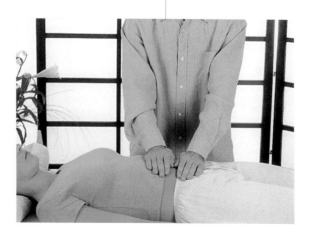

10. Hara/Belly This position can be extended to the sides of the body to include the outer hara.

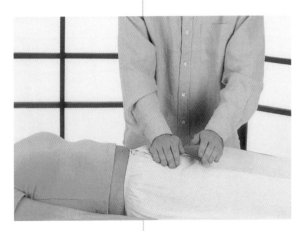

11. Pubic Bone Relates to the second chakra. For the treatment of sexual organs, prostate, bladder, ovaries, urethra, and appendix. Deals with issues concerned with self-worth and creativity, as well as physical, mental, emotional, or spiritual problems due to a misalignment with Mother Earth. In extreme cases, this is the area where suppressed sexual issues, such as rape, abuse, or incest, are stored.

Chakra Harmonizing

Place your hands above the body at the first and sixth chakras, then move your hands together and place them over the second and fifth chakras, before moving on to the third and fourth chakras. Hold each position for one or two minutes, or until you feel the need to move on.

12. Shoulders and Arms Connects the main heart and colon meridians, and helps to comfort the client.

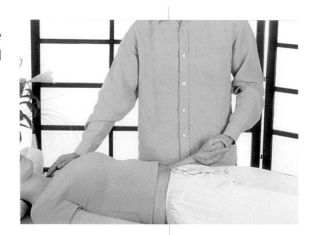

13. Hips and Knees For the treatment of sciatica, arthritis, and joint pains in general. This is another emotional storage area. Stiffness in this region can suggest problems with changing beliefs and moving forward with life.

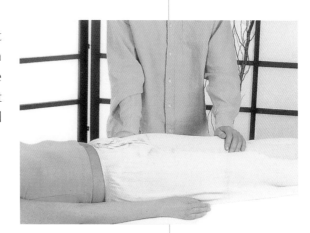

14. Feet These contain meridian points that relate to all parts of the body. Holding the feet helps to ground the client.

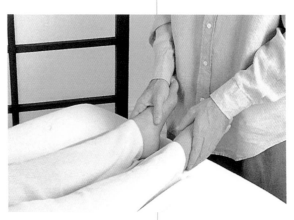

65

Back Positions

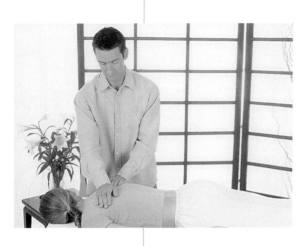

1. Shoulders This position helps to relieve any stress that has built up in this area. The shoulders are where we carry the burdens of other people's expectations of us; our mother's on the left, our father's on the right.

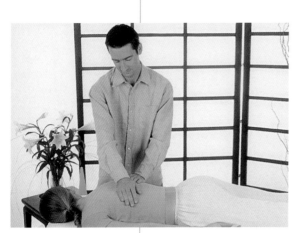

2. Upper Back/Lung Relates to the heart, so the ailments for Front Position 7 apply. This position is also beneficial to clients suffering from bronchial problems.

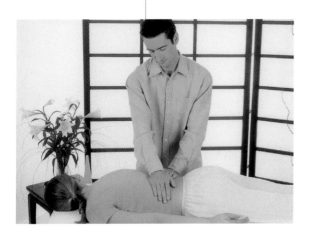

3. Middle Back/Lung Relates to the solar plexus, spleen, liver, pancreas, stomach, and gall bladder.

4. Lower Back Relates to the second chakra, and so the ailments for Front Position apply. Also for the treatment of sciatica. Another emotional storage area.

5. Buttocks Relates to the second chakra. This is an emotional storage area relating to our childhood. Issues such as sexual abuse are often found here.

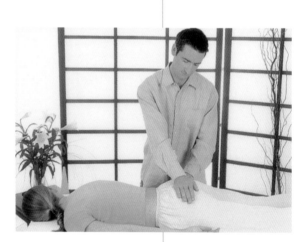

6. Back of the Knees This covers two minor chakras at the back of the knees and helps to ground energy. The knees are symbolic of our fear of moving forward in life.

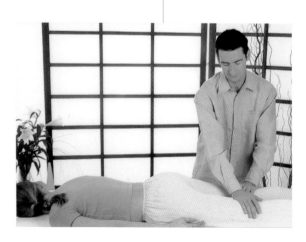

7. Feet This position grounds the client, balancing the whole treatment and grounding energies into the minor feet chakras.

8. Coccyx and the Top of the Spine/ Seventh Vertebrae This position helps energy to run through the spine and removes any blockages that may exist.

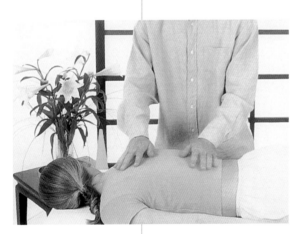

9. Heart and Solar Plexus This final position closes the session and places energy into the heart and solar plexus so that the client will feel centered and empowered.

Checklist For Full Treatment

1. Spend some time preparing your Reiki space with sage or incense to help clear the energy in the room.

2. If you are using a table, prepare it with a covering of paper towel or clean linen.

3. Take a few moments to sit quietly and give yourself Reiki, concentrating on your heart and solar plexus areas to clear your own energy.

4. Your first impressions of your client are important. Often people will not disclose how they really feel, so it is important to trust your own observations. Something that appears quite irrelevant could be the key to the healing.

5. Reiki healers are not doctors and it is important to remind the receiver that we cannot predict the outcome of a healing or work on specific areas. We can only ask for the best for our receiver, and offer the healing as a complementary therapy. Explain this to the receiver, and tell them a little of what you will be doing and what they can expect. Make them as comfortable as possible.

6. Begin by scanning the receiver with your hands and make a mental note of any areas that seem out of balance to you.

7. Having begun the healing, show respect for the receiver's well-being at all times. Try to stay present and focused, and allow yourself to be guided.

8. Encourage any emotional releases and reassure your client that it is OK for them to feel this way.

9. Seal the aura with gentle strokes in an anti-clockwise direction around the full length of the body. Tell the client that they have five minutes to bring themselves round. Wash your hands and fetch them some drinking water.

10. Help your client off the table and check how they feel.

11. Once the client has left prepare the room again. Give thanks to your guides and angels for the help you received and take a break in the fresh air to ground yourself.

12. Check your energy for anything that you feel you may have taken on board and clear it with Reiki before continuing with other treatments.

Short Treatment

The short Reiki treatment has been specifically designed for working in on-site situations where there are time restraints. It can be used in many different situations and you do not need to invest in a proper portable massage table.

Use a chair with an open back, to enable the hands to make direct contact with both sides of the person. The positions have been developed to maximize the available time while still concentrating on the key energetic points of the body. As with the full treatment, begin at the head and work your way down through the main vertical channel of the chakras. The front and back of the chakras are worked at the same time, treating both sides of the same chakra as a whole.

It is important that the receiver is comfortable, and that they take off their shoes and keep their feet firmly placed on the ground. Try to make sure they are sitting upright to prevent any blockage to the flow of energy forming along the spine. Key aspects of the full treatment still apply to the short treatment. For example, the receiver needs to be treated with the same care and attention, they must be in a safe place where there are no distractions, and you need to be sure you will not be disturbed. These factors will allow the receiver to relax into the treatment and benefit fully from the healing.

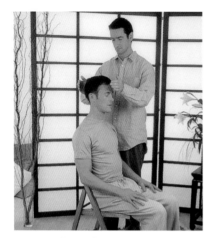

1. Stand at the side and place one hand in front of the third eye and the other to the back of the head. Hold for three minutes. Hold the hand at the front 2–3 in (5–7½ cm) from the forehead, or place your hand over it.

2. Place your hands over the temples, fingers pointing forward. Hands can be held in the aura or kept in contact with the body.

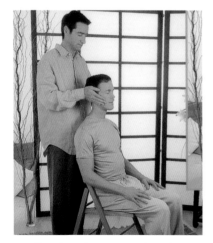

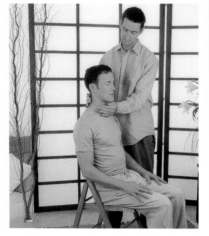

3. Gently place your hand over the ears. The palms of your hands should be cupped over the ears, with fingers pointing along the jaw bone. Hold for three minutes.

4. Place one hand on the back of the neck, holding the other in the aura in front of the throat chakra. Do not make contact with the throat, as this can feel invasive and uncomfortable. Hold for three minutes.

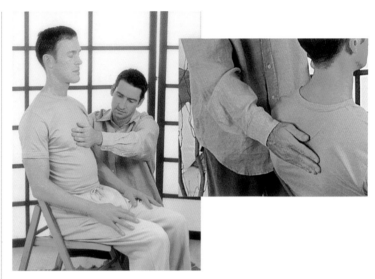

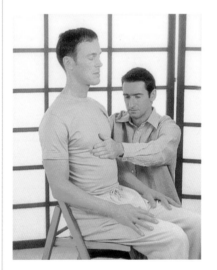

5. Move the hands down, placing the front hand on the upper chest and the back hand on the seventh vertebrae. Hold for three minutes.

6. Place the front hand on the heart, with the back hand mirroring it by working on the rear aspect of the heart chakra. Hold for three minutes.

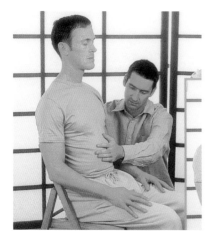

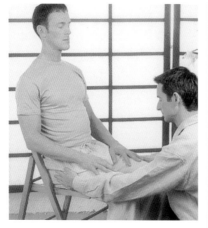

7. Place the front hand on the solar plexus, with the back hand mirroring this action on the middle of the back. Hold for three minutes.

8. Move to the front of the body and kneel down. Place both hands together over each hip. Hold for three minutes.

9. Place both hands over the tops of the feet, helping to ground the receiver to end the treatment. Again, hold for three minutes.

Self-Treatment

Self-treatment is the mainstay of your personal relationship with the Reiki energy. It helps you to maintain your connection, to deepen your relationship with the energy, and to work on a continual basis to clear your own vessel.

Penetrating Heat

On the day after a first degree Reiki course one of my students told me that she had compared the heat of her hands to that from a hot water bottle. She had been amazed at how the heat from her hands had penetrated deeply into her body, whereas the hot water bottle heated only the surface.

This process never stops, and it is advisable to maintain a discipline of working with the self-treatment once a day. The basis of the treatment mirrors that of the short treatment and foundation treatment, beginning with the head positions and working through the main energy centers down the body to the feet. Once you have learned one treatment you will find that others come easily.

During your first encounters with Reiki you will be concerned with your own transformation and healing. However, you will find that as you go further in your work with energy, and start to work on others, this self-treatment plays an important role in maintaining your own energy and keeping yourself clear. With the help of self-treatment you can recognize any changes taking place in your own energy field and clear it out easily and efficiently. By maintaining high levels of ki in your etheric field you help yourself stay healthy and improve your immunity to disease. So you may find that if you come into contact with the flu virus, you can clear away the symptoms energetically from your field of energy. In doing this you may not need to take on the actual physical symptoms.

One of the Reiki master's commitments is to work every day with the self-treatment to keep themselves clear and open. It is important to remember that the treatment forms a foundation that should be referred to whenever you work. However, if you have areas outside this foundation that need to receive healing do not

feel bound by the format of the treatment. In other words, place your hands wherever you feel pain.

The self-treatment is a beautiful way to nurture yourself on all levels. Whatever is going on in your life, this simple and effective technique can provide you with support.

Above: As with other forms of Reiki treatment, begin with an invocation to the Reiki masters and the universal Reiki energy (see page 59).

75

1. Place your hands over your face, with the palms over your eyes and your fingers pointing upward toward your hairline. Keep your fingers and thumbs closed and relax. Hold this position for three minutes.

2. Bring your hands outward to cover your temples at the same height as Position 1. This position can be held with direct contact with the temples or about 3 in (7½ cm) away.

3. Cover both ears with your palms, keeping your fingers together. This is a powerful position to bring a sense of balance to the left and right sides of the brain and body.

4. Place both hands behind the head, in whichever way is most comfortable. This area is connected to the third eye and is regarded as the memory bank for stored emotional memories.

5. Place one hand at the back of your neck and the other over your throat, working on both sides of the throat chakra at the same time.

6. Place one hand on your heart and the other on your solar plexus chakra. This position can be used at any time during the day to help center you.

7. Place two hands horizontally just under the breast, fingers pointing toward each other. This is an important emotional storage point, where we suppress anger.

8. Place one hand on top of the other, covering the entire digestive area. Your hands should face in opposite directions and sit above and below the belly button.

9. Place the hands in a V shape from your hip bone, pointing downward and covering the pubic bone so that your fingertips touch. For women, this is very helpful for the alleviation of pain during the menstrual cycle.

10. Close your hands over your hips.

11. Place your hands over both knees, fingers pointing downward. The knees are areas where we hold resistance and fear about moving forward in our lives.

12. Finally, hold each foot for a few minutes. This action helps you to ground yourself, and treats the numerous meridian points on the feet and toes.

Chapter 4

Second Degree Reiki

"Illness is some form of external searching. Health is inner peace."

COURSE OF MIRACLES

Second Degree Reiki

Involving a deeper commitment to the principles of Reiki, taking you to a new level of understanding.

How Classes are Structured

What to expect when attending a second degree Reiki course.

A Deeper Understanding of Energetics

All of nature is interconnected, so a global understanding of Reiki is essential.

The Three Golden Keys

The secret symbols that unlock the power of healing, discussed in detail.

Distant Healing

Healing energy can be sent across distances using Reiki. You can even "heal" an event in your future.

The Power of Intention

How to ensure the Reiki energy is used as purely as possible.

Developing your Empathic Abilities

Exercises and case studies to help you empathize on a deeper level.

Energy Blockages

Advanced techniques to clear energy blockages using Reiki.

Second Degree Reiki

After the integration period of twenty-one days that follows the first degree initiations students have usually decided whether they wish to gain more skills and understanding in Reiki.

In traditional Reiki a period of three months is required before the student is able to continue on to second degree. This is to allow all the changes that take place in the student's field after the first level time to rebalance and be fully integrated. However, we are all different and this period is, therefore, merely a guideline. Normally, the student and master will determine the correct time to move on to the second degree level.

The intention of the second degree is to make a deeper commitment to healing both ourselves and others. Usually it is those people who have healed their own lives, through awareness and commitment to change, that are the best guides for others to do the same. It is important that those people who go on to second degree Reiki have gone some way toward understanding their own process, and have understood the help Reiki has given them in that process. They must see the journey forward as a means of self-development, as well as a route to help others.

During the second degree course the student is introduced to the three key Reiki symbols, as shown to Dr. Usui on Mount Kurama in Japan. Each symbol has a specific function, and during the two-day course the student will learn the importance these symbols have in future healing work. Issues held on emotional and mental levels can rise up into our consciousness and, through the skills we learn on the course, we are able to work on these at a far deeper level. Second degree Reiki introduces the student to powerful new ideas,

Below: Rose

As you go on to study second degree Reiki, your understanding and healing ability will develop and blossom like a rose.

making them more aware of the connection to all that is. We begin to understand that the past, present, and future can all be accessed in the now.

We learn to use that connection to heal our present situation by sending healing to wherever the issues originally occurred. This opens our awareness as we learn to connect to our own childhood, for example, or to people from our past who still affect us in some way. We are introduced to the ability to send energy across distance, learning that we are not restricted by space. We can connect to people, places, or situations and support them through the healing power of Reiki, wherever they may be. This then introduces group work and the power of sending energy to places of crisis in the world. Through exercises we learn to focus our intention and, through the unlimited nature of Reiki, send love to wherever it is needed.

Above: The two horizontal lines in this symbol, given to the author in meditation, represent the two planes of existence, spirit and earth, and the vertical line symbolizes the journey between the two.

Left: To progress to second degree Reiki, you must show a deeper level of commitment, as in marriage, to healing yourself and others.

83

How Classes are Structured

The second degree course is usually held over two days, during which time students are introduced to the three second level symbols.

T he meaning of each symbol is discussed in turn, the students being invited to give their own perceptions of each symbol. I am always amazed at the accuracy of their perceptions, and encourage these to be shared before giving the traditional view.

After the symbols have been shown they are empowered through an initiation. Only one initiation is given on the second degree course. This initiation is designed to empower the symbols given to us, the belief being that without the initiation the symbols have

Right: Photographs of loved ones can be used for distant healing: Reiki can be sent over distance to friends and family.

little power or meaning. This is the reason why some masters have felt justified in publishing the symbols in books or on the Internet. The traditional view is that the symbols are secret and should remain so.

The course is structured around the symbols, with exercises given to demonstrate how they work. These involve the emotional and mental healing technique and distant healing techniques. I also devote time to group sharing of each individual's experiences since completing the first level. It often helps to consolidate each person's experience when they hear of other people's journeys.

I ask the group to bring in photographs of themselves as children, as well as photographs of friends or family. These are used in distant healing exercises connecting to the person in the photograph and sending healing to them.

Above: Try using boxes to test your distance healing. You can place objects or photographs of loved ones in them, in order to focus your healing powers more strongly.

I also devote time to increasing the students' awareness of their own energy field through self-awareness exercises, thus increasing their empathic abilities.

Students learn the importance of setting up the healing space, how to clear a space of negative energies in preparation for healing, and how to prepare themselves for a treatment. At the end of a treatment they are taught how to clear their energy.

By the end of the course the students feel confident in their knowledge of the symbols and how they are to be used. They should feel confident in their ability to hold a space for another to receive Reiki and be able to cope with any emotional releases that may occur as they work. They will have a growing trust in their intuitive abilities and in the energies they are working with. They will also have a deeper commitment to their own personal growth and transformation with the help of Reiki.

Second Degree Reiki:

Your course should include:

- The three symbols and their uses.
- Mental and emotional healing.
- Group healing.
- Distant healing work.
- Lots of group hugs.

A Deeper Understanding of Energetics

As we begin to use the Reiki treatments we have learned, it is interesting to observe the range of people we attract. Nothing ever happens by chance, so it is often helpful for us to note the issues carried by those people we treat.

Often other people's issues will reflect those that we still hold ourselves and are working on, or issues we have resolved in our own lives. This places us in the perfect position to help them with their own process as we draw on our own experience.

I have often seen that people who carry very similar issues are brought together. Either they share similar experiences and so are able to empathize with each other, or they operate from a place of polarity observing how their own behavior may be affecting another.

When a person releases a long-held issue it can begin a chain reaction within the group. Others will also release similar issues that they hold, or observe the suffering their actions may have caused in others. It is as if the group has tuned into a particular frequency that represents an issue and anyone who carries that issue in their field begins to be affected.

If this can take place within a group then it also holds true that as we begin healing issues individually, the effect of that healing may be felt globally by everyone who holds that issue within their field. The idea that a butterfly flapping its wings can cause a tidal wave on the other side of the world follows the same principle. This is a powerful concept and one that I encourage my students to embrace. If we accept that we are all one then any shift taking place anywhere affects us all, no matter how small that shift may be.

I saw this principle take effect in the most intense way when

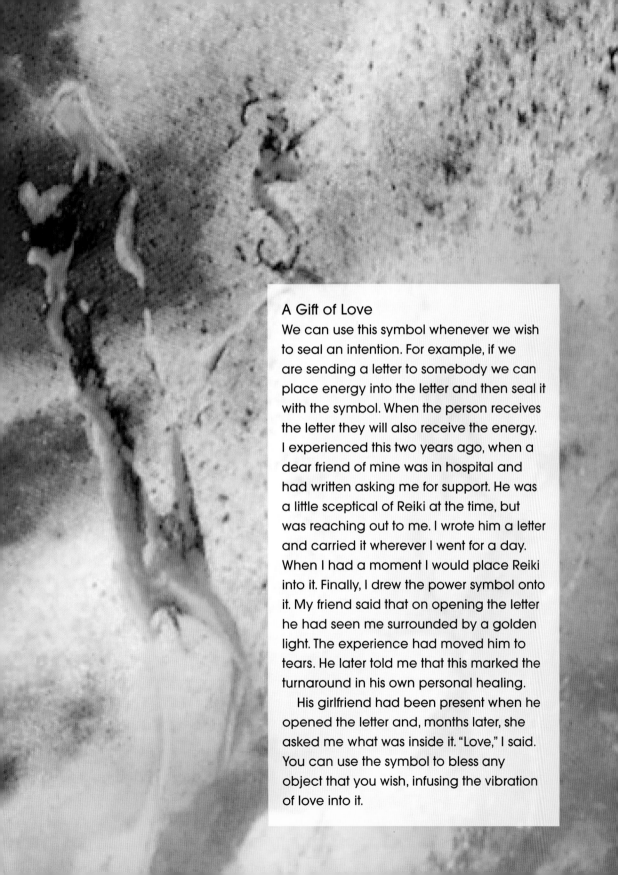

A Gift of Love

We can use this symbol whenever we wish to seal an intention. For example, if we are sending a letter to somebody we can place energy into the letter and then seal it with the symbol. When the person receives the letter they will also receive the energy. I experienced this two years ago, when a dear friend of mine was in hospital and had written asking me for support. He was a little sceptical of Reiki at the time, but was reaching out to me. I wrote him a letter and carried it wherever I went for a day. When I had a moment I would place Reiki into it. Finally, I drew the power symbol onto it. My friend said that on opening the letter he had seen me surrounded by a golden light. The experience had moved him to tears. He later told me that this marked the turnaround in his own personal healing.

His girlfriend had been present when he opened the letter and, months later, she asked me what was inside it. "Love," I said. You can use the symbol to bless any object that you wish, infusing the vibration of love into it.

Emotional Mental Symbol

Element WATER
Mantra Translation NATURE, HABIT

The second golden key is to the doorway between the physical, emotional, and mental bodies. The symbol is comprised of left and right, representing the masculine and feminine aspects, and comes from Sanskrit, symbolizing the Tibetan goddess of mercy.

I t is connected to the element of water, which helps us to understand its action. Water is deeply connected to our emotional nature, working to restore harmony between the physical, mental, and emotional bodies. It helps us to remember emotional memory, beliefs, or trauma that may be held in the physical body and the field around it. This memory will often relate specifically to a period of our lives where discomfort or trauma was experienced which, though suppressed, still affects our lives in unconscious ways. It enables us to release these emotions or traumas.

Below: First degree Reiki is an introspective journey into the self, away from the crowd.

In addition, this symbol can also help to resolve present-day conflicts or emotional trauma that may occur as a result of an accident or surgery. It works on the mental body in releasing old patterns that no longer serve and may be standing in the way of healing on other levels. It can be drawn into an area that is detected as "out of balance" at any time during healing.

A specific healing technique, unique to this symbol, is called emotional and mental healing. This is a simple use of the symbols drawn specifically into the third eye. This healing is deeply profound and can be the key to unlocking dreams for the future, as well as issues from the past.

Unlocking memories

I experienced an example of the emotional mental symbol's power in a recent second degree workshop. I had introduced the symbol and asked the students to sit with it and see what they felt. Within seconds one of the students started to cry and said she couldn't continue looking at the symbol. She had seen images from her childhood that she had forgotten: the symbol had literally unlocked the memory and brought it into her awareness again. This is a powerful way to resolve issues. In her case, she went on to express the anger she felt and has gone some way toward healing that particular emotional scar.

Distant Healing

Element SUN
Mantra Translation TRUE MEN NEED PURE HEARTS

The third of the golden keys is to the doorway that takes us outside of time and space. It symbolizes the universal part of us that can reach out to all that is. With the help of our intention it connects us to a person, place, or situation etherically, allowing the Reiki to flow from source to wherever it is needed.

This symbol is primarily used to send Reiki over distance, and is used in group work to send energy to situations, people, or places that require healing. It can be used to connect to someone who is too far away to arrange a normal session but requires healing to help them through a difficult period. It can also be used to send energy to a situation or event that requires healing, such as peace talks between nations or conflicts on a national scale. Most people find this concept acceptable in terms of their own belief system. They might have had the experience of thinking about someone moments before that person calls them on the telephone. Or they may have felt uneasy when thinking of a friend, only to discover that the person has been going through trauma of some kind. The idea, therefore, that we can connect to another and send healing energy to them is within the realms of possibility for most people.

Through the use of this key we are able to go outside of time and connect to any place we choose for the purpose of healing a situation. For example, if we are able to go back to a point in time when current issues and pain were created, then we are able to trigger the release of the issue in the present. During the second degree course I guide the group through a healing that involves going back to a period in childhood. By using the symbol we send energy to that time to release any issues that are held.

94

Energy Over Distance

I have had many experiences of distant healing. Most have simply involved experiencing a warm cloak of energy descend on me as other Reiki practitioners have sent energy to me. I was to do a presentation recently in Italy and some of my students had come by the house beforehand to talk. I felt unusually nervous so went upstairs to spend some time preparing myself. While I was in meditation I felt a huge wave of energy sweep over me and instantly I felt calm and at ease. I went downstairs to find my students in a circle holding hands. They felt me coming in and opened their eyes. "We were just sending energy to you," they said. "I know," I replied, "I have just received it."

Distant Healing

Above: To help you visualize and focus on the intended recipient of your distant healing, look closely at a photograph of them before sending the Reiki.

Sending Distant Healing

When sending distant healing it is important to create a space that enables you to open up to Reiki without fear of being disturbed. If possible, the recipient should be aware of the time you will connect to them so that they too can utilize the energy to the best effect. Go through the procedure of invocation and preparing your space as if you were doing a session one-on-one. I will usually combine a self treatment with distant work, working first on myself and then spending time to connect with others. This way I am focused and centered in the energy and can be of more benefit to others.

Light a candle and sit facing it. If you have a photograph of the person place it near the candle so that you can focus on them. If not, you can visualize them or write their name on a piece of paper and place it next to the candle. An object belonging to the person can also be used to form a connection. If you have the second level symbols then use the sequence your master taught you.

If you prefer, you may try this sequence, which is very powerful and is the sequence I teach:

- Name of person three times.
- Power symbol three times.
- Mental, emotional symbol three times.
- Power symbol three times.
- Distant symbol three times.
- Power symbol three times.

Once drawn or visualized, take a breath and blow through the palms of your hands, visualizing the person or simply focusing on the photograph or object you have in front of you. You then simply hold your attention on the person for approximately ten minutes. With practice you will be able to feel the emotional space the person is in and even the physical symptoms they are carrying. The simplest way to do this is by working through the chakras one at a time and registering how your own chakras respond.

Using the same procedure, you may send distant healing in the

"We may be brothers after all. We shall see..."

CHIEF SEATTLE

same way to an event in your future, such as an important exam or interview. Instead of a person, focus on the event that you wish to send energy to.

Above: Blow the energy through your palm chakras, while holding an image of the recipient in your mind.

Working as a Group

When we work with a group our power is multiplied by the number of people in the group. Many different projects can be chosen by the group and these should be clarified before beginning. The group should sit in a circle facing each other with a candle placed in the middle. Each person in the group can nominate an individual and provide a photograph or object of that individual, placing it into the center of the circle. If the group decides to work on a political issue or a recent disaster, such as an earthquake, then that intention is placed into the circle. It helps to have an individual nominated to focalize the group, taking them into the healing and then bringing them out again. The same procedure is followed as before. All members of the group draw the sequence of symbols and together blow the energy into the center of the circle. Hold the focus for ten minutes and then gently bring the focus back to the room.

Below: Use a personal object to connect you to the time, place, or person you wish to send healing to.

Afterward the group can share their individual experiences.

Above: One of the advantages of Reiki is that it allows you to beam energy across distances.

Beaming Energy

The sequence of symbols I have given on page 88 can be used to beam energy at whatever you choose. A useful group healing exercise for this is to create a circle and lay someone down in the center of it. Make sure they are comfortable and warm. Then, from a distance, the group draws the sequence and directs the energy at the person lying in the center. Again, this need only be for ten minutes. When the healing is over the person nearest the person's feet simply moves forward and takes the feet in their hands to ground the person. The reaction to this exercise is always amazement as the recipient feels as if they are floating, supported by an energy blanket of love.

The group can then discuss what they felt before the next person lies in the center.

Working on Specific Issues

Using the distant healing symbols we can target specific issues that prevent us moving forward. For example, we may have issues relating to jealousy or possessiveness that continue to surface in our lives. Even though we are aware of them they prevent us from experiencing happiness and joy in our relationships. We can use Reiki to bring about shifts in our perspective and the way our conditioned responses to a situation cause us to act. It is better to deal with issues one at a time so that you do not over-extend yourself.

You will need a lighted candle and a fireproof dish for this exercise. Once you have decided which issue you wish to work on write it down on a piece of paper and sit with it. Examine what the issue means to you. For example, what is jealousy to you? How does it make you feel? What does it look like in someone else? What other times in your life did you feel jealous? Now think of an affirmation that will empower the release of this issue, such as "I am releasing the patterns that create jealousy in my experience". State out loud the affirmation three times. Draw the sequence of symbols to empower your affirmation then light the piece of paper with the candle, place it in the dish, and allow it to burn. Repeat this once a day for seven days.

Left: You can also practice Reiki over the telephone, sending healing remotely. The recipient can experience this as a rush of heat similar to that experienced in one-on-one Reiki.

Above: Write out the issue on a piece of paper, empower it with symbols, then release it by burning it.

Using the Telephone

Due to time constraints I am not always able to do one-on-one healing. I find that I spend a lot of time talking through problems with people on the telephone. This modern-day tool is a very simple way to connect to somebody and get a sense of what they are experiencing emotionally. With practice you can empathize just as easily over the phone as if the person was standing right in front of you. I will, therefore, use the telephone to connect and simply use the symbol to send healing wherever it is needed. I will often guide the person through the healing on the other end of the phone at the same time. It is a very straightforward and powerful way to work.

99

The Power of Intention

When the first level students are asked to comment on their experiences, they talk about how different the experience of giving Reiki can be, depending on the situation.

I f they go through the set procedure to prepare the space, the healing seems more powerful than if the students just lay their hands on somebody without any preparation. Here they are discovering the power of intention. It is the intention we bring to everything we do that is communicated on an energy level. Whether it is cleaning the bath or giving somebody a massage, it is the intent and focus we bring to the task that will affect the final result.

Right: A safe environment for the receiver is created if you "seal" the space before starting the Reiki session.

Placing a clear intention into the space I work in is one of the most important aspects of working with energy for me. Once I have done the preparation I feel supported and guided. It is as if a warm jacket of supporting love descends around me and I am transported to another level of being, where my perception, awareness, and sensitivity is taken to a heightened state. I feel I am operating from a place of wisdom, and I know I am completely safe and so is anyone entering the space.

After completing the preparation sequence outlined on the right, you may feel presences either side of you, and heat or vibration on the side of your face and down your arms. These are the guides who will assist you in your work.

Use the remaining time available to sit quietly with your hands over your heart and solar plexus so that you are open and aware of how you feel. When the receiver arrives they are usually very aware of the difference in the energy of the room. Sometimes simply entering the room is enough to facilitate an emotional release.

Negative Intention

I have experienced the power of intention during a massage. I was lying on the table, without clothes on, feeling vulnerable and putting my well-being in somebody else's hands. The practitioner was distracted and not entirely present. I left the massage with an overwhelming sense of not being appreciated or cared for.

As a rule, good practitioners are very professional and usually that professionalism will include awareness of the importance of being clear and focused in intention.

Preparation

- Arrive thirty minutes before the healing is to take place.
- Spend a few moments feeling the room, to get a sense of what has taken place earlier.
- Light a candle with the intention of dispelling darkness.
- Burn frankincense and carry it around the room with the intention of clearing the space of all blocked energy. As you do this you may feel a flood of heat coming into your hands and around your shoulders.
- Place the power symbol into one corner of the room. Draw the energy along to the next corner and, again, place the power symbol into the corner. Repeat until all four corners are sealed.
- Seal the entrance to the room with the power symbol.
- Sit quietly and make your invocation. Call on the Reiki to descend all around you, cleansing and purifying everything within the room. By this time the room will be completely charged with Reiki.

Developing Your Empathic Abilities

Much is made of the gift of seeing energy fields or being clairvoyant, but another gift is more available to everyone and is one of the most accurate tools we have when working with energy.

Empathic Predictions

An interesting aspect of being empathic is that the healer will often feel something before the recipient. They may say: "Are you feeling a pain in your right kidney?" "No" replies the recipient. A few minutes later they will begin to feel pain in the right kidney! These days when the recipient says "No, I don't feel anything in the right kidney", I usually reply, "You will in a while!" The sceptics among you will say that this is auto-suggestion. However, years of experience have shown me that bringing awareness to an area can reveal hidden issues.

This is our ability to empathize or to be empathic. The process of initiation in Reiki increases our personal awareness and, therefore, our capacity to empathize. With guidance, a student can become aware of his or her capacity to empathize and develop it as an accurate tool in a relatively short period of time.

To be truly effective, a healer will always have to experience a certain amount of the recipient's pain. This may be felt in many ways, ranging from a wave of emotion to small sensations in the hands as they are passed from position to position. It is not to be confused with taking on someone else's pain. All these sensations are often an accurate reflection of what is going on in the recipient's energy field or physical body. In time, if we allow ourselves to explore these experiences, they will serve to alert us to what is happening in the recipient.

Empathy is a tool that can be honed and perfected to assist you in your work. It will help you discern what is going on energetically in someone you are treating. It is quite common for people to respond to the question of how they are with automatic responses such as, "fine, thanks". At the same time, they may be tied up in knots inside of themselves. It is, therefore, important to develop your sensitivity so that you can see through the illusions that people present to you. This will prove

will slowly clear the area. Sometimes, however, a little help is required. There are several techniques we can try.

Pulling Blocked Energy out of the Field

We can use a simple pulling technique to encourage the energy to break up and be pulled from the field of the recipient. When you feel a block in the energy field allow your hand to gently move up and down over the area, feeling for the tension point. This is a little like making energy balls in the palms of your hands. When you feel the tension slowly pull your hand out of the field, making sure the tension is maintained. Once you are away from the field, throw or flick the energy directly into the earth. Never throw it horizontally across a room, or in the direction of someone else, or the energy will contaminate their field. Go back to the same spot and repeat as many times as necessary until you feel the area is clear.

Above: Creating a connection between two points using the fingers will cause energy to flow between the points.

Spine Clearing

One of the most common blockages is along the spinal column. This carries the main vertical power current designed to ground energy from spirit. Blockages can occur anywhere along the length of this vertical column, depending on which chakra is being affected at any given time. However the common point that seems to build up pressure is at the base of the neck. This is a common cause of pressure buildup in the head which leads to headache and migraine. The blockage may occur lower down but the pressure backs itself up to this point. To clear, place one finger at the base of the neck and another at the base of the spine. Simply relax and let energy trickle between the two points. The recipient will normally feel this trickle of energy as it travels through the spine and they will sometimes spasm as the block is rapidly released through the energy channels. This feels a little like an electrical shock.

107

Laser Techniques

In addition to sending energy from the hand chakras it is possible to use your forefinger and index finger to channel energy. This is especially useful if you wish to be specific in highlighting an area that is blocked. Lightly place your fingers on the area and relax. The Reiki will route itself through them into the recipient's body. Recipients report feeling as if my finger is actually going right through them and moving things around inside their body. This is a useful technique to open up the heart and solar plexus when blocked.

Right: Use your fingers as "lasers" to specifically focus on an area.

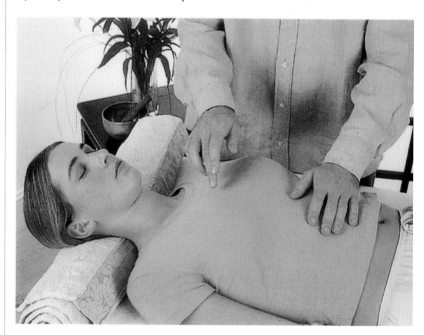

Energy Break Up

Sometimes energy blocks need a little encouragement to begin breaking up. In much the same way as a massage therapist will knead the stiff muscle in order to encourage it to relax, so we may employ a similar technique to encourage energy to break up. This technique is done by spreading the fingers of the hands and shaking them from side to side over the blocked area in a rapid movement. This technique is especially useful in the solar plexus and hara area, where energy can become very knotted and stuck. Once the energy begins to move, return to the original method of laying your hand on the area.

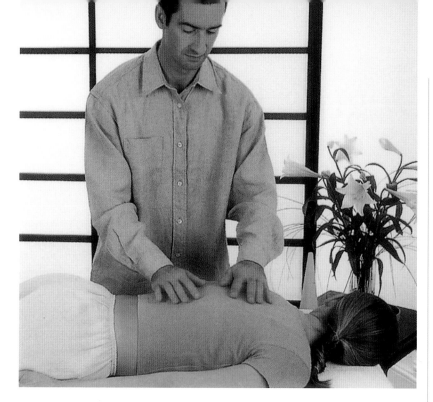

Left: Shake the hands in a kneading motion to break up solid blocks of energy, especially in the solar plexus.

Breath

Breath is your greatest ally when it comes to breaking up old stuck emotional issues. Often a person will be reluctant to breathe into areas that are stuck or stagnated and the breath will appear shallow and weak. Ask the person to open their mouth and breathe in deep, fast breaths, in and out of the mouth. Place your hand on the area you wish them to breathe to and support them by matching your breath with theirs. As the area affected is oxygenated old emotions within the cells begin to shift and the person will find that the body takes over the breath control—it becomes automatic. The person will often experience a release of emotions and tingling sensations in their hands as the block begins to move. This technique is quite dramatic and reassurance must be given to the recipient so they feel secure and safe throughout. Once the emotion has been expressed the person will feel very light and free. Allow them to relax for some time and keep them warm with extra blankets. Go to the feet and use the Reiki to ground them.

Below: Encourage the patient to breathe correctly to stimulate blocked and stagnant areas.

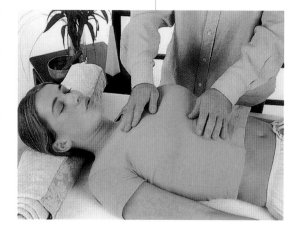

Third Degree Reiki

The third degree Reiki course, or master level, is designed for those people who wish to fully embrace the principles of Reiki into their lives, and teach others these principles.

The title "master" simply means that a person has received the final initiation in the Usui system of natural healing and has completed all aspects of that system to a level of understanding, which means they can pass it on to others. The master will, hopefully, have learnt enough on his own inner journey to recognize and help others overcome possible pitfalls. The term "master" can be misleading, implying that a person has mastered all aspects of their life. This is not necessarily the case, and discernment is required when choosing a Reiki master.

There are certain criteria that a student will have to fulfil in order to participate in the master training. These criteria differ depending on which master you choose, but essentially follow similar guidelines. A master looks for people who have the attributes to make a sympathetic teacher and have embraced the principles of the teachings into their own life. They should have a good understanding of Reiki, practice regularly, and possess the courage and eagerness to continue growing.

At this level, the student-teacher relationship becomes very close. Often the student will work alongside the master on a one-to-one basis for a year or more, providing the perfect opportunity to learn the skills necessary to work with groups and pass on the

"In the life of the spirit, you are always at the beginning."

RALPH BLUM

Free as a bird
Once you have been initiated as a Reiki master and have run a first and second degree Reiki course under supervision, you are free to teach and heal alone.

teachings. A financial exchange will take place that reflects the time the master devotes to the student.

The master initiation is usually received over a weekend. Again, how the course is structured depends on the master you choose—some take students to sacred sites or places of significance to make the initiation more memorable. The structure of the weekend should involve receiving the master symbols, the single initiation, and instruction on how to pass on the attunements. A commitment is agreed between the master and student on the work that is to follow. This will include assisting the master in his or her courses, passing on attunements, and helping to organize sharing groups or doing administrative work.

111

When the student master is ready they will teach a course themselves with supervision. Once the student master has successfully run a first and second degree course they are then free to teach alone and are considered a Reiki master. In order to maintain the high standards of Reiki masters, it is important that this apprenticeship is honored.

The master level, like all the stages of Reiki, is a beginning rather than an end. Often a person's choice to become a Reiki master will coincide with big shifts in the way that person chooses to live their life. The choice to become a Reiki master is a choice to assist others in realizing their full potential as human beings.

The Financial Exchange

Below: In the traditional Usui system, money is seen as energy. One unit of money, in any currency, equates to one unit of Ki.

The traditional Usui system considers the financial exchange to be part of the master initiation. This figure was arrived at by Hawayo Takata, the last grand master. At the time it equated to $10,000, which in Japan is seen as a sacred number, though the amount has obviously grown with inflation. It was felt to reflect the student master's understanding of living in an abundant universe where they were able to create what they needed. In other words, if you really believe that you create your own reality go and create $10,000.

This has attracted a lot of criticism from the non-Reiki community, who argue that if Reiki is given to the universe why should we pay for it? But who gave us the trees, the water, the minerals, the flowers, the land, our bodies, or the earth itself? Charging for these things is considered justifiable because they are more tangible.

The issue here is not about paying for Reiki, but rather how we view money, which is merely a form of energy. It has no value of its own, it is simply a form of exchange designed to equate to the energy either given or received. Receiving the master initiation and teachings is a gift of universal proportions and the cost, in comparison, seems quite insignificant.

Holding a Space for Healing

When working on another person it is important to remember that they are facilitating the healing, not the healer. It is very easy to fall into the trap of believing that, as healers, it is our power and expertise that creates the shifts and transformations in others.

Opposite: Through the recognition of another's pain and suffering, we develop compassion. As we watch them heal, a part of us heals with them.

Nothing could be further from the truth. It is true that some healers have high awareness, making them more alert to the needs of the person they are treating. This helps them to act at the right time, encouraging the recipient to let go of whatever issues they are holding. But the healer him or herself be cannot physically release these issues. Nor can we force people to go through doors that they are not yet ready for.

When we are alert to another person's situation we are in empathy with them, we are listening. If the recipient is aware of this they will feel supported and he more prepared to work on painful issues. Our responsibilities as healers are simply to listen, open our hearts, and hold the quality of stillness as we channel Reiki. In doing this we hold a space within which another person can transform. The Reiki will be the force that the person uses to create the necessary shift in vibration within their physical, emotional, and mental bodies and, if ready, they will then be able to release whatever they are holding. It is vital that they take responsibility for their own healing to avoid dependency on the healer.

Below: Once you have been initiated as a Reiki master and have run a first and second degree Reiki course under supervision, you are free to teach and heal alone.

Chapter 5
The Seven Chakras

"Negative and detrimental thoughts can grow as fast as weeds in a garden and choke all beautiful and delicate flowers if they are allowed to take control."

EILEEN CADDY

Understanding the Seven Chakras

If areas of the body's energy field are blocked, a physical disorder can be caused. The Reiki practitioner can use the chakra system as a key to discovering and healing these blockages.

Understanding the Seven Chakras

Reiki looks at disease from an energy standpoint, searching for areas in the energy field that are blocked and restricting its flow to the physical body.

The Reiki healer sees these blocks as a form of pollution in the energy field, often the result of unresolved negative emotions or thoughts. We concentrate on the chakra system in order to understand why a disorder exists and create a positive energetic shift. As we have learned, these energy centers relate to the emotional and psychological make-up of a person, as well as to the physical body. The chakras are like a map of a person, holding the history of all that has happened to them and offering dues for helping their healing.

Often, several chakras are holding pollution and operating dysfunctionally all at the same time. A negative loop of experience is then set up, as each dysfunctional chakra affects the others.

The Negative Loop

Trust is a basic psychological theme for the first chakra, the negative aspect being mistrust. If we partner this with a theme from any one of the six other chakras we can see how they coexist to form a dysfunction, leading to a negative experience of the secondary chakra characteristic. For example:

- **Sexuality:** Lack of trust linked with sexuality could lead to a negative experience of sexual intimacy.
- **Identity:** Lack of trust linked with identity could lead to an unbalanced view of the Self.
- **Trust and love:** Lack of trust linked with love could lead to an inability to give and receive openly.
- **Communication:** Lack of trust linked with poor communication could lead to a restriction in the ability to express feelings.

- **Intuition:** Lack of trust linked with intuition could lead to a lack of faith in one's own perception of others.
- **Union:** Lack of trust linked with union could lead to a pessimistic view of one's place in the universe.

As a rule, the first three chakras are the main source of negative pollution in the energy field. This is because the first twenty years of our lives are formative times, when we are strongly influenced by outside influences. Any buildup of negative pollution in these three chakras will, in turn, have a negative effect on the chakras that we have yet to develop.

The following pages contain a series of affirmations combined with natural mandalas, which can be used to affirm your relationship with your chakras.

First Chakra: Muladhara

*I am safe, I trust in
the natural flow of life.
I take my natural place
in the world, content in
the knowledge that all
I need will come to me in
the right time and space.
I am secure and grounded
in the physical form and
give thanks to Mother
Earth for the nourishment,
shelter, and stability
she gives me.*

Second Chakra: Svadhisthana

*I am a sensuous being.
I express my sexuality fully
and freely in all I do.
I celebrate the creative
exchange of sexual energy
in the universe.
I honor the union and
integration of the masculine
and feminine principles as I
recognize and integrate these
principles within myself.
I give and receive freely from
the wellspring of life.*

Third Chakra: Manipura

*I am at peace with myself
and my surroundings.
I express my identity without
imposing my will upon others.
I see the differences in others
as unique expressions that
contribute more color and
fragrance to the world.
I am energized by the light
and heat of the sun.
I am in harmony
with all I see.*

Fourth Chakra: Anahata

*I am motivated by selflessness.
I cultivate the quality of
compassion for myself and
all sentient beings.
I have the willingness to
transform pain and suffering
in others with the
knowledge that, as I do,
I transform pain and
suffering within me.
I have the courage to
love unconditionally.*

Fifth Chakra: Vishuddha

I am free to express my creativity with unrestricted enthusiasm and joy.
I give voice to my feelings and communicate with clarity and openness.
I am a unique being, my opinions are of great value, and I share them fearlessly.
I am imaginative and colorful in all I do.

Sixth Chakra: Ajna

*I create my own reality.
All experiences that I come
into contact with are a
reflection of my own projected
thoughts and emotions.
I develop my inner senses.
I am open to new ideas and
spiritual concepts.
My intellectual mind
recognizes my intuitive
perception.*

Seventh Chakra: Sahasrara

I contemplate the impermanent nature of reality. I release attachment, recognizing that it is the source of all suffering. I develop emptiness so that I may experience union with the universal consciousness and merge with the oneness of all creation. I am content.

Muladhara: The First, or Root, Chakra

Significance and function The first chakra is our most basic—standing for the core of our being and connecting us with our group identity. It is about security and the desire to remain safe—teaching us to look after ourselves. It tethers us firmly to the ground, just like the roots of a tree, and is the starting point for the energy rising up through the other chakras.

Location	Perineum and the base of the spine
Bodily connections	The genitals, spine, hips and pelvis, the adrenals, the skin and skeletal system, legs and feet, elimination system
Themes	Survival and security, self-preservation and fight or flight, home and belonging, having one's feet on the ground
Colors and hues	Rich reds and yellows
Element	Earth
Balanced or unblocked	Grounded energy and good health
Unbalanced or blocked	Self-destructive, lacking in energy and drive. The person may suffer from foot, bowel or bone problems
Symbol	Downward-pointing triangle set in a red square framed by four lotus petals

Svadhisthana: The Second, or Sacral, Chakra

Significance and function   The second chakra is connected with our sensual selves, helping us to connect with the qualities that enhance our lives. This chakra is all about our sensuality and sexuality, and the need for us to access our emotional sides. It is the pleasure center that can allow us to become true creative beings, connecting with our enjoyment of life.

Location	The area of the genitals and the navel
Bodily connections	The testes and ovaries, digestive organs, kidneys and urinary tract, circulatory system, womb and prostate
Themes	Pleasure and "sweetness" and the central life concept of "Who am I?"—a question which may be answered through using personal creativity and exploring relationships, intimacy, sexuality, food and appetite
Colors and hues	Oranges and reds
Element	Water
Balanced or unblocked	Natural joyful expression of sexuality and the sensual side of life, feeling good about life in general
Unbalanced or blocked	Sexual and fertility problems, kidney and bladder problems, and health problems associated with the womb, ovaries, and prostate. There may be pessimism and emotional coldness
Symbol	A lotus with six petals containing a white circle to represent water and a crescent moon

Manipura: The Third, or Solar Plexus, Chakra

Significance and function   The third chakra is concerned with personal power and strength, and someone who is balanced in this area displays a well-rounded personality and is at ease with the whole world. They have good self-control and exercise willpower with the aim to succeed.

Location	The solar plexus area
Bodily connections	Stomach, liver, adrenal gland and gall bladder, spleen, digestive system
Themes	This is the center of one's own wisdom and power over one's Self
Colors and hues	Yellows
Element	Fire
Balanced or unblocked	Feelings of quiet strength and the ability to contribute to the common good. If things stand in our path, this doesn't faze us. We have quiet confidence that we can work for the good of all
Unbalanced or blocked	Digestive problems and diseases such as cancer and anorexia. A domineering personality may display itself
Symbol	A lotus with ten petals surrounding a downward-pointing triangle

Anahata: The Fourth, or Heart, Chakra

Significance and function   The fourth chakra relates to self-nurture as well as to the care of others. It comes midway between the lower, grounding, chakras and the higher, more spirit-led, chakras. The love experienced in this center is without conditions and contains generosity and giving.

Location	At the heart level of the chest
Bodily connections	Heart, lungs and respiratory system, chest and circulation, hands and arms
Themes	The love that moves outward to others and inward to the Self
Colors and hues	Green and pink
Element	Air
Balanced or unblocked	When a person lives through their love and makes their acts of compassion and empathy work for others
Unbalanced or blocked	Heart problems such as heart attacks, immune system problems. Hard-heartedness may be a trait
Symbol	A twelve-petaled lotus holding a star made of two intersecting triangles

137

Vishuddha: The Fifth, or Throat, Chakra

Significance and function   This chakra is concerned with communication. It encourages us to speak out and allows our creative selves to flourish.

Location	The throat
Bodily connections	The voice and throat, neck and jaw, mouth and teeth
Themes	The focus of a person's ability to show their connectedness to others and to let them know what lies within. Self-expression and communicating ideas are keynotes
Colors and hues	Blue
Element	Ether
Balanced or unblocked	A clear voice and great ease of communication. We love to hear what this person has to tell us
Unbalanced or blocked	A sore throat might indicate a reluctance or inability to communicate or express what is within. Otherwise, thyroid problems and difficulties with the vocal cords, nose and ears may be associated. If someone can't stop talking, their throat chakra may be malfunctioning
Symbol	Sixteen petals surrounding a full-moon circle

Ajna: The Sixth, or Third Eye, Chakra

Significance and function   This chakra is about connection with absolute clearness of mind in the use of intuition. There is the potential to unlock psychic abilities.

Location	Between the eyebrows
Bodily connections	Pituitary gland, eyes, face
Themes	Looking within and interpreting what is found there. Using intuition and the imagination to expand and delve into all that is. Exploring consciousness
Colors and hues	Indigo blue with hints of yellow
Element	None
Balanced or unblocked	Wisdom emanates from someone who operates with this chakra functioning well and others love to learn from them
Unbalanced or blocked	There is an over-rationality about this person and they pay little heed to spiritual life. Headaches may be a feature of this form of dysfunction
Symbol	A two-petaled lotus

Sahasrara: The Seventh, or Crown, Chakra

Significance and function The seventh chakra is our highest. It focuses on the spirit, in which we can attain our ultimate potential as spiritual beings. The main quality is of enlightenment and fulfilment in all things.

Location	At the crown of the head
Bodily connections	Brain, pineal gland, the entire body
Themes	Oneness and utter bliss, when we are at one with the cosmos
Colors and hues	Violet and white
Element	None
Balanced or unblocked	A life lived in spiritual practice may guide the person toward enlightenment
Unbalanced or blocked	Focusing on the material world may prevent a progression toward the spirit. Depression is one symptom
Symbol	A thousand-petaled lotus

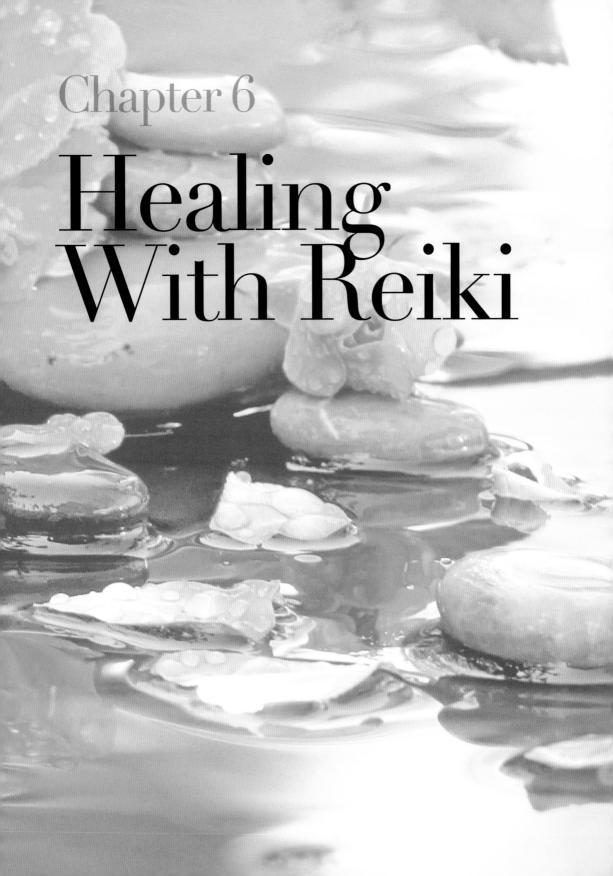

Chapter 6
Healing With Reiki

"It is health that is real wealth and not pieces of gold and silver."

MAHATMA GANDHI

How to use Reiki to help heal and get over a range of the commonest ailments, both physical and mental.

Colds, Flu, and Headaches

Allergies

Bronchitis and Asthma

Insomnia

Stomach Aches

Menstrual Problems and Menopause

Neck, Shoulder, Back Problems and Sciatica

Eye and Ear Problems

First Aid Techniques

Healing Emotional Difficulties

Healing Destructive Anger

Healing the Spirit with Reiki

Colds, Flu, and Headaches

Colds and flu, with the familiar symptoms of a runny nose, cough, and perhaps headache and fever, visit us all too frequently throughout the year, though they are most prevalent during the damp, cold months. They are the body's response to viruses and are a way of getting rid of toxins and waste matter.

Above: To help a headache, treat the back of the receiver's head. Cradle their head in the palms of your hands, with your fingertips on their medulla oblongata.

Viruses may strike when you are feeling at a low ebb, and when your body does not have the resistance to fight them off. Perhaps you are going through a spell of being run down, tired, over-worked, and being generally out of sorts.

Take Time Off

If you can, it's a good idea to stay off work and rest, to avoid spreading infection around your workplace or on public transport—or to avoid picking up further infections yourself. You'll get better faster if you can really take time off to rest properly, and you can try some Reiki treatments in the peace and quiet of your own home, without disturbance.

Think about your diet because it could be making your cold or flu symptoms worse. Try cutting out or reducing the amount of dairy foods, such as milk, yogurt and cheese, you are having, and take on board as much fluid as you can. Try hot lemon and honey drinks, herbal teas, or just plain water, to flush out your system and keep you well-hydrated.

Try not to take medication that suppresses the symptoms, but you may find that taking vitamin C and multivitamins does help. If you need to, take pain-relief medicine to get you through the worst phases.

If your nose is badly congested, making breathing at night difficult, try a steam inhaler to clear your nasal passages. Keep as warm and cosy as you can, either in bed or wrapped up well on the sofa—and try to relax as much as possible.

Healing at Home

Try the following Reiki self-healing sequence on yourself—it is especially effective for helping colds and flu. Hold each position for a few minutes before moving on to the next. Try the exercise either sitting up or lying down—whichever feels more comfortable. You can do the sequence first thing in the morning and then last thing at night, and you will find it effective if you have a headache, too.

- Gently place your hands over your eyes, so that your palms rest lightly on your cheeks.
- Now move your hands to your temples, so that your palms rest just above your ears.
- Then put your hands on your head, with your palms covering your ears.
- Move your hands so that they are holding the back of your head.
- Now move your hands to gently hold your throat on either side. If you have a sore throat, this should feel soothing.
- Lastly, put your hands on your chest, just below your collarbone, with the tips of your fingers just touching. This will help to strengthen your immune system. You can hold this position for a little longer than the others.

If it feels more relaxing and convenient, ask another person to carry out the Reiki hand positions on you (they will need to be a Reiki practitioner). You can lie down and relax more completely, letting your mind float. It is not necessary for the giver to touch you, the receiver—their hands can be placed a little way over your body, in contact with your aura.

Below: You'll be doing yourself, and others, a favor if you stay at home and rest. You'll recover more quickly and avoid passing on your cold or flu to others.

145

Allergies

An allergic reaction occurs when the immune system responds inappropriately to a trigger. Symptoms can be anything from the sneezing and runny nose of hay fever—a result of inhaling pollen— to rashes caused by contact with substances that irritate the skin.

Above: To treat allergies, place your hands over the upper part of the receiver's face, a short distance away. This position balances the pineal gland and stimulates and balances the sixth chakra, helping the person to relax.

Just breathing in pollen on a summer walk in the countryside, or eating a "trigger" food, can accidentally affect us in ways that may vary from the mildly irritating to the downright dangerous. Allergies affect people at different times of their lives; you may suffer from an allergy in childhood, but gradually grow out of it as the years go by, or you may be surprised to start suffering from hay fever in your middle years, when it has never affected you before.

What You Can Do

If you know what is causing your allergy, then you can do your best to avoid contact with the irritant—or in the case of foods, stop eating whatever is triggering your allergy (provided you know what it is). For example, peanuts are a common culprit and are relatively easy to avoid. It's vital to be aware of recipe ingredients if you are not cooking the dish yourself and, in the case of children, you need to teach them how to avoid the culprit food when they are not with you—say at a birthday party.

It's important to read food labels carefully when shopping, and enquire in restaurants about the precise contents of a dish before you decide what to order. Eggs, strawberries, seafood, food colorings and preservatives may cause violent allergic reactions, and persistent symptoms may be caused by intolerance to wheat if you have celiac disease.

If you suffer from allergic rhinitis as a result of pollen and dust mites you should avoid contact with animals, use synthetic pillows and mattresses on beds, keep your home as dust-free as possible, and avoid walking in long grass or on newly mown lawns.

It is not always obvious what is causing an allergy problem, so you may need advice from your doctor and to undergo testing to pin down the culprit. Skin-prick tests are a common way to identify allergens. These test are simple and painless and a reaction may occur within minutes, informing you whether you are allergic to that substance or not.

To assist the detoxification process it will help if you drink plenty of plain, still water every day.

Left: Pollen and dust mites can cause an allergic reaction, which results in sneezing and a runny nose.

How Reiki Can Help

Try giving yourself a Reiki session for ten to fifteen minutes per day to help the detoxification process and clear any blockages. Ask someone else to give you Reiki healing (a first-degree Reiki practitioner) so that you can lie down and relax more fully. The giver's hands can either be a short distance from your body or be in full contact. Either method can be calming and effective, so choose the one you prefer.

- As the giver, place your hands over the receiver's eyes, on either side of the nose, fingertips pointing downward, so that their forehead and cheeks are covered. This position will help to unblock the sinuses, if necessary.
- Form a T-shape with your hands over the receiver's chest—your hands should be at right angles to each other. This position helps the immune system and the lungs.
- Place your hands horizontally on the receiver's waist to treat the lymphatic system and help clear toxins away.
- Now put one hand horizontally on the upper chest and the other horizontally on the left side of the lower rib cage.

Bronchitis and Asthma

Bronchitis occurs when the bronchi become infected and this is largely brought about through breathing a polluted atmosphere and through smoking. Asthma is also inflammation of the bronchi, which causes the airways to narrow, making breathing difficult, causing the person to become breathless, with wheezing and coughing.

The result of bronchitis is debilitating coughing, which produces phlegm. The breathlessness can be alarming. The condition often starts in childhood, but ceases as the person grows to maturity. However, some adults suffer throughout their lives. Asthma may be preceded by continuous colds and bronchitis.

Helping Bronchitis

The best possible plan to help bronchitis is to stop smoking—if you do smoke—and avoid passive smoking as well. If you have to spend time near smokers, either ask them to move to a different area or move away yourself. It's a good idea to drink plenty of fluids throughout the day and to use steam inhalations to clear your nasal passages before you go to sleep.

Above: Placing both hands on the upper back, horizontally, one behind the other, helps lung disorders, coughs and bronchitis.

   Try the following Reiki hand positions to help bronchitis:
- As the giver, put your hands in a T-shape on the receiver's chest—one horizontally and the other vertically.
- Now lay your hands horizontally on the chest, one behind the other. If direct contact is not desired, you can treat the aura space by holding your hands a short distance above the chest.
- Work your way down the chest and abdomen—holding your hands horizontally, one behind the other, so that the fingertips of one hand just come into contact with the palm of the other.
- Now ask the receiver to turn over onto their front and place your hands on their upper back, horizontally, with one hand behind the other—in the same way.

Relieving Asthma

Asthma attacks are triggered by different things in different people, but very often they are characterized by undertaking vigorous exercise, exposure to dust or pollen and cold, damp conditions, plus feeling stressed—and combinations of all of these things. For example, if a susceptible person playing at a sports fixture is feeling nervous on a cold, damp day, then the conditions could be conducive for an asthma attack to ensue.

If asthma attacks start in childhood or as a teen, then homeopathic treatment can be very effective and the attacks can be stopped. It's a good idea to cease consuming dairy products and cut down on animal protein and avoid tea, coffee and alcohol if possible.

Try this Reiki treatment to help asthma.

- As the giver, cradle the receiver's head with both hands, with their fingertips over the medulla oblongata. This will help to calm their emotions and allay fears. It is also effective if the person has a headache.
- As the giver, place your hands in a T-formation on the receiver's upper chest. One hand is horizontal and the other is vertical. This position treats the thymus gland and lungs.
- Now place both hands on the chest horizontally, side by side, to treat the upper lungs.
- Position one hand on the upper breast/chest horizontally and the other on the middle of the abdomen, toward the left side.
- Now, on the receiver's back, place your hands on the lower back at the waist, horizontally, one behind the other.
- Using the same hand position, move down to the waist and rest there for a few minutes.

Above: It is important that everyone takes exercise and team sports are a great choice for all. If asthma is controlled properly then exercise should not be an issue.

149

Insomnia

We all have different sleep patterns. Yours will depend on your age and stage in life. For example, hormones may affect the quality and patterns of your sleep. The menopause is a time of life when many women experience insomnia—perhaps for the first time in their lives.

Although the usual length of time for a good night's sleep is reckoned to be six, seven or eight hours, many people can survive, and even thrive, on a lot less. Insomnia is when usual sleep patterns have become disturbed and you find it hard to get good-quality sleep. Perhaps you fall asleep easily enough at first, only to wake up a few hours later and find it difficult, perhaps even impossible, to get back to sleep again.

Common Causes

You may be disturbed by unfamiliar light in the room or noises, your brain may be unable to switch off from the preoccupations of the day, or your body may feel uncomfortable and restless. These effects can all be made worse if you are sleeping in an unfamiliar place. Other causes include eating and drinking, especially alcohol and coffee, too late in the evening, suffering from depression or being seriously worried about a specific issue (see also pages 186-7).

Right: Work out what is causing your insomnia, so that you can resolve any issues and enjoy a good night's sleep.

However, if the period of insomnia goes on for too long, your overall health may be affected and you may find it hard to concentrate during the day, feel irritable and bad tempered, and experience difficulty dealing with ordinary tasks. In addition, your physical health and immune system may be affected and you may become prone to developing colds and flu (see also pages 144-5).

Things You Can Do

It's wise not to have a meal within three or four hours of retiring for the night, and it's best to avoid coffee and other drinks in the evening. Make sure that you take plenty of exercise during the day—lack of it can make you feel twitchy and restless. If possible, go for a brisk walk for half an hour every day.

Perhaps you could try to develop a calming ritual before you go to bed. You could have a long, soothing bath, perhaps adding a few drops of relaxing aromatherapy oil to the water and lighting some atmospheric candles. In your bedroom, open a window, just a little, to allow fresh air to circulate. Keep lighting dim. Think about whether your bed could be made more comfortable—is it in the best position in the room, are your pillows right for you and your sleep habits (too soft, too hard, too high, too flat) and is your bedding of the correct thickness for the season? Read a calming book before you turn off the light—one that is not too challenging and stimulating—and refrain from watching television. You could try using a herbal pillow with lavender in it, or burning a calming aromatherapy oil on the bedside table.

Calming Reiki Routines

While you are preparing for bed, try this quick and easy Reiki exercise to get you in the mood for sleep.
- Sit up or lie down in bed—whichever feels most comfortable.
- Close your eyes and breathe as slowly and calmly as possible.
- Place your hands beneath your opposite armpits.
- Direct all your attention inward, toward the center of your chest.
- Let an atmosphere of restfulness come from your heart.
- Remain in this position for up to fifteen minutes.

151

Stomach Aches

Stomach aches may be caused by a variety of physical problems, including indigestion, food poisoning, constipation, irritable bowel syndrome, and menstrual problems.

Alternatively stomach aches can be caused by a build-up of tension and stress, which can be held in the stomach area, producing aches and pains. A common manifestation of this is when an anxious child claims to have a tummy ache on a school day.

Indigestion

Indigestion is a common complaint that can be caused by eating too rapidly, consuming too much, or eating food that is too rich. Stress can make the complaint worse. The pain is often known as "heartburn" or is experienced as an ordinary stomach ache or as feelings of nausea. The best way to avoid it is to eat simple, plain food and plan healthy food combinations. You could try eating proteins and carbohydrates at separate meals and eat fruits and puddings separately. If you are prone to suffering from indigestion, it's best to avoid meats, fried foods, dairy products and sugar altogether.

The following Reiki treatment may help—though you will need to ask someone else (a Reiki practitioner) to carry it out on you.
- As the giver, place your hands on the receiver's ribs and waist, on the right side, to treat the digestive areas.
- Now place your hands on the receiver's left side.
- Then position your hands just above and below the navel to treat the stomach and intestines.

Diarrhea and Constipation

Diarrhea is usually the body's response to a toxin in the digestive system, resulting in passing watery stools frequently. It is important to be aware that fluids and salts are lost rapidly from the body and should be replaced quickly. So if you suffer a bout, be sure to drink as much water as you can and avoid eating or drinking dairy products,

Above: Lay one hand on the receiver's solar plexus and the other on the heart. This treats the solar plexus for digestive problems and the heart for stress-related problems.

eating plums and apricots and indigestible foods. The same Reiki positions can be used as for indigestion (see left) and may be very helpful. Constipation is usually a result of eating a low-fiber diet, so it is a good idea to eat plenty of green, leafy vegetables, whole grains, and raw fruit, and drink lots of water. Try the following Reiki hand positions—ask someone else (a Reiki practitioner) to perform them on you.

• As the giver, place your hands horizontally across the receiver's waist, around the navel, with the fingertips of one hand touching the palm of the other.

• Treat the colon area by placing your hands in a V-shape, with one hand pointing upward, the other downward, over the pubic region.

• Put both hands over the receiver's lower waist on the left side to treat the spleen and pancreas.

Irritable Bowel Syndrome (IBS)

IBS causes a great deal of discomfort, but it is not usually serious. Both diarrhea and constipation can be symptoms. It is usually possible to help calm the symptoms through choosing what you eat carefully and dealing with any stressful life issues as effectively as you can. It's best to avoid eating large meals, dairy products, coffee and tea, and foods that contain grains such as barley, wheat and rye. Try the same Reiki treatment as for diarrhea and constipation for the relief of pain.

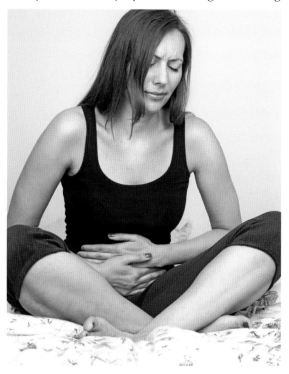

Left: Avoiding trigger foods and stress can help relieve the symptoms of IBS.

Menstrual Problems and Menopause

Some women are fortunate enough to go through life without ever suffering unduly from either menstrual problems or menopause symptoms, while others suffer a great deal of pain and discomfort.

Painful periods are relatively common, though the reasons for them are not fully known about. The menopause can start at any time from your mid-forties or early fifties and is signaled by the gradual cessation of monthly periods.

Painful Periods

Other issues, such as missed periods, may be due to stress or inadequate diet (or even pregnancy), while excessive bleeding may be due to hormonal balance. Both need to be checked out by your doctor. If you experience tenderness in your breasts before a period, irregular periods, or very heavy bleeding, you may have higher-than-average estrogen levels. It's wise to see your doctor for specific advice.

To give yourself a Reiki treatment for menstrual pain, try the following self-treatment positions.

• Position your hands over your pubic bone in a V-formation with the fingertips just touching.

If someone else (a Reiki practitioner) is available to treat you, try the following Reiki positions.

• As the giver, position your hands over the receiver's pubic bone in a V-formation, but with one hand pointing downward and the other pointing upward.

• Place your hands right next to each other on the receiver's waist on the right side.

• Now put your hands on the opposite side of the receiver's waist.

• If the receiver is experiencing troublesome back pain, ask her to lie on her front and place your hands across her lower back, letting the fingertips of one of your hands connect with the palm of the other.

- Put your hands into a T-shape on the area at the base of the spine. The left hand should be placed horizontally across the receiver's lower back, with the right hand positioned vertically to it. Let your hands rest there for a few minutes.

Helping Menopause Symptoms

The menopause can be seen as an important change in a woman's life, and perhaps even as a positive marker indicating the start of a new phase of life. There may be symptoms such as night sweats, hot flashes, sleeplessness and disturbed sleep patterns, and vaginal dryness, as well as general feelings of being emotional and moody. Some doctors recommend hormone replacement therapy (HRT), while others only advise it for a limited time. Osteoporosis and higher blood fat levels can also result from the menopause.

Above: Regular exercise is an excellent way to relieve the symptoms of the menopause.

It is important to take plenty of regular exercise at this time of life—either regular gym sessions, dance classes, yoga or tai chi. A brisk daily walk for half an hour is ideal. Aim to eat a diet that is low fat and rich in fiber content, and avoid eating too much red meat, fats, sugars, and refined foods. Avoid drinking alcohol and coffee as much as you can, and focus on boosting your intake of fresh fish, fruit, and vegetables. Try the following Reiki treatment, asking someone else (a Reiki practitioner) to treat you.

- As the giver, position your hands over the receiver's pubic bone in a V-formation, but with one hand pointing downward and the other pointing upward.
- With the receiver lying on her front, place both hands above the waistline on the left side, hands touching each other.
- Now place your hands in the same configuration, but in the center of the back, just above the waistline.
- With the receiver lying on her back, position your hands in a V-shape over the pubic bone again.

155

Neck, Shoulder, and Back Problems and Sciatica

We are all prone to channelling stress into the upper back, and tend to hold a lot of tension there. This can bring about sore neck and shoulder muscles, as well as back pain.

I n addition to holding on to stress, emotions and responsibilities, bad posture and pain can be worsened through long hours spent sitting in front of a computer, and perhaps poor chair and desk height, as well as being an incorrect distance from your computer screen. If you are unfortunate enough to suffer from sciatica, you will know that the pain running down the leg caused by a trapped nerve can be excruciating. You need to consult your doctor, and possibly a chiropractor, before looking into Reiki healing.

Neck and Shoulder Pain

It is a good idea to try to pinpoint exactly what is causing your neck and shoulder pain, and then take steps to improve your working environment. Take regular daily exercise, such as a visit to the gym or a bracing walk, and make a point of getting up from your desk at frequent intervals to stretch, walk about, and have a change of activity. Pain can also be caused by other repetitive postures and actions, such as always carrying a heavy shoulder bag on the same side.

Try the following Reiki positions to help your neck and shoulder pain. You'll need to ask someone else (a Reiki practitioner) to treat you.

- As the giver, position one hand at the nape of the receiver's neck and the other at the top of the spine.
- Then move your hands so that they are next to each other, over the left shoulder blade.
- Shift your palms to the right shoulder blade, over the spine.

Back pain

There are all sorts of reasons for back problems, ranging from holding on to tension, or eating a poor diet, to lifting a heavy load in an awkward way, standing in an awkward way for prolonged periods, or driving for lengthy spells. If possible, try to find out the main cause of your back problems and take steps to alleviate them. For example, if you sit a great deal in daily life, try to move about at regular intervals. See if the following Reiki positions help.

- As the giver, position your hands on the receiver's back, just above their waist, with your hands placed horizontally, one butting into the other.
- Repeat the position, but slightly lower down the receiver's back.
- Now, carry out the same position on the lower back over the hips.
- Then place your hands in parallel on either side of the lower spine—one hand facing toward the receiver's head, and the other toward the feet.
- Finally, balance the back energy by placing one palm on the lower back, fingertips toward the head, and the other across the nape of the neck.

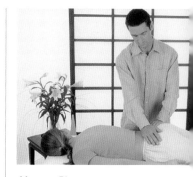

Above: Place your hands across the coccyx area, one hand behind the other. Much emotional energy is stored here.

Helping Sciatica

A few Reiki positions may calm and soothe the pain. Ask someone else (a Reiki practitioner) to carry out the positions on you, while you lie on your front. It may help to rest your lower legs on a flat pillow.

- As the giver, position one hand over the base of the spine, with fingers pointing toward the feet and the other, in parallel, with your fingers pointing toward the receiver's head.
- Now place one hand horizontally on the base of the spine and the other at varying positions on the back of the thigh, between buttock and knee.
- Move one hand to lie on the back of the knee and move the other gradually down toward the heel.
- Place one hand below the knee and the other on the underneath of the foot, with your fingertips pointing toward the toes.
- Now perform the same positions on the other side of the receiver's body, working down their other leg.

157

Eye and Ear Problems

The eyes and ears are delicate organs, and so you should visit your doctor or optician if you are experiencing persistent problems. However, Reiki can be used to calm and soothe some of the more minor ailments such as eye tiredness and buzzing in the ears, and it has been shown to be very effective.

Above: Place your hands in the aura over the eyes and cheeks to treat eye problems. As well as being relaxing, this also stimulates and balances the sixth chakra.

Resting your eyes at regular intervals can help relieve tired eyes, especially if you use a computer as a regular part of your working day—it's all too easy to sit in front of it for long periods without noticing, and your eyes tire very easily. There are many infections that can affect the middle ear, the ear canal or inner ear, causing excruciating pain, or you may suffer from earache caused by flu or tonsillitis. If you are prone to build-ups of wax this may cause partial deafness, pain and tinnitus—a ringing or hissing in the ears—which is very hard to live with if it is loud and persistent. Your balance may also be affected by ongoing ear problems. If you have earache or ear problems that do not go away quickly, see your doctor.

Dietary Advice for the Eyes

It's a good idea to cut down on meat, dairy, and stimulants such as tea, coffee, and alcohol and stick to a good, basic healthy diet containing whole grains and vegetables high in beta-carotene. You can test out the old adage about carrots helping you to see in the dark by eating lightly steamed carrots, or drinking carrot juice.

Eye Relaxation Sequence

Try this sequence if your eyes are tired and it will help to relax your whole body, too. You will need to ask another person (a Reiki practitioner) to perform the healing on you.

- The receiver should lie on their back with the giver seated at their head. As the giver, place your hands on either side of the receiver's nose so that their forehead, eyes and cheeks are covered. In this way you will bring about a balancing of their pituitary and pineal glands.

- Place your fingertips very carefully on the closed eyes, with index fingers in contact with the inner corner of the eyes.
- Now lay your hands over the temples, palms following the head shape and fingertips touching the cheeks. This position treats the eye muscles.
- Cradle the back of the receiver's head in your palms to ease tension in the eyes and calm eye disorders.
- Place your hands next to each other on the lower abdomen to treat the liver—the liver meridian runs through the eye.

Above: Position your hands in the aura over the sides of the temples to treat the optic nerves and balance the right and left sides of the brain.

Dietary Advice for the Ears

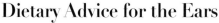

It's sound advice to avoid wheat and dairy products as well as meat. Instead eat steamed vegetables, citrus fruits, and rice.

Tinnitus Relief Sequence

Lie down flat and ask another person (a Reiki practitioner) to perform this exercise on you to relieve tinnitus.

- As the giver, place the hands on either side of the receiver's head, covering the ears completely. This helps the receiver relax and calms down hissing noises.
- Now move your hands to the jaw on either side, also covering the ears.
- Place the palms behind the ears, leaving your thumbs in front of the ears.

Left: Ear problems can have several causes, but lifestyle changes, especially dietary changes, may help to relieve them.

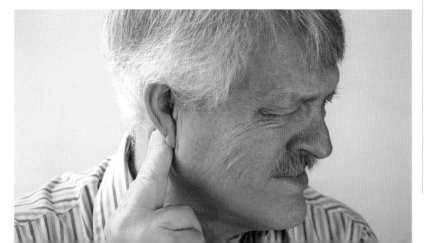

Reiki First Aid Techniques

Reiki probably isn't the first thing you think of following an accident, but it can be used very effectively to help calm the injured person while you are waiting for emergency help to arrive—and after first aid has been administered.

Above: Reiki can help to calm an injured person and aid their recovery, but respect their wishes if they do not want you to use it.

Adrenalin courses through an injured body, creating panic and stress, but Reiki can really help to get the healing process started by de-stressing the body. If the person is in shock, reduce the effects by calmly laying your hands on the back and front of their body; if they cannot be moved, simply hold their hands, unless these are injured.

Always call emergency services first—before you start to administer Reiki—and do not try to move the person if they cannot get up (unless it is necessary to remove them from further harm). Cover them gently with a spare coat or rug, and support their head if this is possible. If the person is upset they may not want to receive Reiki, so be sensitive to their wishes. Never force Reiki on anyone if they do not want it.

Self-Treatment with Reiki

If you have had an accident, you may be able to treat yourself, while awaiting emergency help, and after you have received first aid—to assist the healing process. This is particularly appropriate in the case of a sprained ankle, for example. It is reassuring to know that you cannot overdo Reiki. You can use intuition about where it is best to put your hands—Reiki will flow from your hands and your own healing power will make it effective and help to strengthen the receiver. When you first start treating yourself, you might initially feel worse, but this is quite a normal reaction. The best plan is to persevere with Reiki as it will certainly help you to recover more quickly.

160

Shock Following an Accident

Try laying your hands on the person's third chakra, and then on their shoulders. If they seem fearful, try laying your hands on the third chakra area and the back of the head simultaneously to try to calm them down.

Breaks, Bruises, and Sprains

Do not touch a suspected broken bone before emergency services have assessed it. This is because Reiki can accelerate the healing process and the bone will need to be set, or the sprain examined and treated, before you give healing. Once the bone has been set (if necessary) you can give Reiki by laying your hands over the cast. You can place your hands gently over a bruise and give Reiki for up to half an hour. The same applies to sprains, though you can give Reiki for longer and keep repeating the treatment in this case.

Burns and Insect Bites

Try giving Reiki around the injured area for short periods of about twenty minutes—in mild burns this may have the effect of reducing blistering. If burning is severe you must not touch the area at all until after first-aid treatment has been given, and the area dressed. Then it is wise to only treat the aura over the burn. If someone sustains an insect bite you can give Reiki directly to the area for up to half an hour, which may help to reduce any swelling.

Heart Attack

While you are awaiting emergency help you can give Reiki to the person's stomach area, but without touching the heart area.

Wounds

Wait until a bad wound has been medically treated before you give Reiki—this is because Reiki can speed up the healing process and in the case of a treating a serious wound (with stitching and/or reattaching a limb) speedy healing caused by Reiki could impede the initial treatment. You can give Reiki to the wounded area after the dressing has been put on, by putting your hands gently on it or in the aura above it.

161

Healing Emotional Difficulties

We all go through times of feeling upset, depressed, and in need of healing and emotional refreshment. There may even be times when we feel quite desperate for help of some kind.

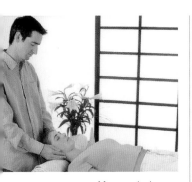

Above: Let your hands rest lightly over the receiver's ears.

No matter how bad these times seem, perhaps it's useful to remember that they do have a purpose—on a very basic level. Perhaps without them we would not be able to appreciate the good times so much. There would be no sense of balance in our lives. However, Reiki can really come into its own when helping to heal emotional dysfunction. Just the laying-on of hands, whether your own or someone else's, can help to dissolve cares and bring comfort to the spirit.

During difficult times it is even more important to care for yourself tenderly. Eat a good, balanced, healthy diet and make sure you get plenty of good-quality sleep and exercise. That way, you will feel better prepared to face your difficulties. There are other things that may help, too. Perhaps you could give yourself a treat of some kind, go out with a friend, pamper yourself—even a long, luxurious bath will do you good.

How Reiki Can Work on Emotions

Reiki can be a very soothing, healing method during times of emotional difficulty. Specific outcomes cannot be predicted, since Reiki works on the areas where it is most needed—it flows as a positive, healing energy source from the giver's body, out through their fingertips, and into the receiver's body.

Worry and upset seem to create a build-up of negative energy that collects in the head area, so a Reiki treatment that focuses on the head will do you a great deal of good. The following exercise helps to balance the hormones, affecting the pituitary and pineal glands, and enables calm to engulf the mind. You'll soon find that your feelings of tension will melt away and you can let go of your most troubling concerns. You will need a Reiki partner (a Reiki practitioner) to treat you, and each position will take about five minutes to carry out.

- The receiver should lie flat on the floor, with a small pillow supporting their head.
- As the giver, sit cross-legged at the receiver's head. Position your hands over their eyes, resting the palms gently on their cheeks.
- Now lay your hands on either side of their head, just above the ears and touching the forehead.
- Position the hands right over the ears. The receiver will feel comforted and loved.
- Now cradle the receiver's head in your cupped hands. Their fears will float away, as if by magic.
- Now move around to the receiver's side and place your hands in a T-position over their chest.
- Put one hand on the receiver's stomach, and the other on their forehead.
- Lay your hands along the insides of the receiver's thighs—position one hand pointing toward the receiver's head and the other toward the feet.
- Put your hands on the receiver's knees horizontally. The worst fears can be released like this.
- Ask the receiver to lie on their front and rest their head on their folded arms. Put your hands on their lower back, horizontally.
- Move to sit beside the receiver's feet. Place your hands over the soles of their feet, with your fingertips pointing toward the floor.
- Now put one hand on the back of the receiver's neck (on the medulla oblongata) and the other horizontally on their back at waist level.
- Finally, moving up and down the length of the receiver's body, smooth out their aura.

Below: The support of a friend who is a Reiki practitioner can be a great help in times of trouble.

Healing Destructive Anger

Many people let themselves down badly when they are unable to control angry feelings. Those who use anger to intimidate others and control them are often, quite simply, bullies displaying unacceptable behavior.

Above: Learning how to deal with your anger will improve your interactions with other people.

Although you may feel a release in the moment of venting your anger, later you may feel ashamed about your display and regret the way you lost control. Your behavior may not help you put your argument across, perhaps the reverse, and you may damage relationships with others.

It's fine to be angry and sometimes to express it, but often an angry outburst in frustration releases the anger while allowing the whole situation to escalate in a damaging way. This may be hard, if not impossible, to recover from—and you may make permanent enemies. However, "bottling up" angry feelings may internalize negative energy, which then finds expression or a "way out" in depression or illness.

What Causes Anger?

Anger often arises because a person feels defensive and wants to lay blame on another. You may feel that others expect things of you that you are unable to deliver, so you feel guilty and defensive as a result. Anger may even have become a habit for you—your first way of reacting to something that upsets you.

Reiki can help us to recognize our own difficult emotions beneath the surface and deal with them safely and calmly. These angry feelings can then be turned around and channeled in a more positive direction. Contemplate the second of the five spiritual principles of Reiki (see pages 166–7) and consider meditating on it daily. (See also pages 218–19.)

Use Reiki to balance your, sometimes overpowering, feelings and let them work "for" you rather than "against" you. You'll find that your nervous feelings calm down. If you feel like crying, don't be afraid to let go and express yourself in this way. The giver (Reiki practitioner) should hold their hands in position and support you until you feel calm again.

How Reiki Can Calm You

- The receiver should lie down, close their eyes, and relax by taking a few deep breaths.
- As the giver, sit at the receiver's head and place your hands on the top of their head, leaving a gap in the center. Your fingertips should point toward their face.
- Put your hands on the receiver's throat, but do not actually touch it—just float your hands over it.
- Move to the receiver's side and put one hand on the side of their waist horizontally and the other further up.
- Now form a T-shape with your hands below the collarbone.
- Then put a hand on either side of the receiver's navel.
- Form a V-shape with your hands and place your hands over the receiver's pubic bone. Your hands should face in different directions.

Self-Treatment

If you would like to treat yourself, try this technique:

- Place one hand on your forehead and the other behind your head, at its base.
- Now put your hands gently around your throat, with your wrists in contact with each other in the center. Have your fingers pointing backward.
- Position your left hand beneath the left side of your back—about halfway down. And put your right hand over the left side of your front.
- Put both hands on your chest—one above the other—the lower one over your stomach.
- Make a V-shape with your hands in your groin area—over the pubic bone.

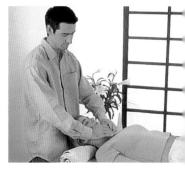

Above: This pose relates to the fifth chakra and can help dissipate anger and difficulties with expressing yourself.

165

Healing the Spirit with Reiki

We are all progressing on a life journey that can give us enormous spiritual richness—if we allow it to. We need to let the light in and be open to our own development and healing.

Reiki can heal emotional hurts, but it can also help keep you focused on the lessons you can learn from misfortunes. Reiki is an important discipline that you can practice every day. You can learn to accept the difficulties of life or perhaps see ways of changing them, or be grateful for the things that do turn out well. Reiki can help you with that loving acceptance.

The Five Principles of Reiki

Use these five principles (see also pages 218-19) to help you focus on Reiki teachings every day of your life. Read each principle in turn before spending a few moments meditating on it. If you make this part of a daily practice, every morning, the day will be imbued with meaning and will turn out better for you. If you are challenged on any of these five principles during the day, return to a moment of stillness within and contemplate moving beyond negative emotions and embracing the positive aspects of life.

- Just for today do not worry
- Just for today do not anger
- Honor your parents, teachers and elders
- Earn your living honestly
- Show gratitude to everything

Finding Meaning in the Five Principles

You can interpret these words in different ways and focus on the ones that speak to you most. "Just for today" tells you that you should live mindfully, in the present moment and not get too distracted by

166

memories of the past and concerns about the future. Focus is in the "now", in which you can act and have influence if you choose to. Doing this, you will soon find that you appreciate your life more and more as time goes by.

Worrying can be a destructive activity (see also pages 186-7). It taps straight into fears about what might or might not happen and sometimes we use it to control the actions of others. Therefore, it can be useful to put your worries aside. If you can, do something to avert, solve, or deflect the thing you are worried about, then do so, but do not waste energy worrying without taking action. Anger is also a highly damaging emotion (see also pages 164-5), which we often use to injure others. Trying to dissipate anger is helpful, so it is worth reminding yourself of this every day, so that you remember not to use it unnecessarily.

Honoring others is worth a daily alert—this is not so much about feeling reverence for elders and betters, but a general respect and sense of value for others and the things they do, whether they affect you directly or not. Earning your living honestly needs no explanation—but perhaps it's good to have a daily reminder of the need to work and live with integrity at all times. And lastly, being grateful is an important precept—allowing you to enjoy life all the more and contribute to it, too, for the good of all.

Connecting to Your Inner Wisdom

Reiki can open your heart to your own wisdom and let you explore the possibilities of your inner life.

- Relax, either sitting or lying down, and breathe deeply—in and out—watching your breath.
- Notice any areas of tension present in your body and relax them one by one, starting at your toes and working gradually upward to your head.
- Place both hands on your heart area and focus your attention there.
- Contemplate any problems or difficulties that you have been experiencing recently. Lay them open before your heart.
- Contact the wisdom of your heart and communicate with it directly about your problems. Ask questions, if necessary.
- See whether any answers surface for you.

167

Chapter 7

Using Reiki Through the Day

"The best things in life are nearest: Breath in your nostrils, light in your eyes, flowers at your feet, duties at your hand, the path of right just before you. Then do not grasp at the stars, but do life's plain, common work as it comes, certain that daily duties and daily bread are the sweetest things in life."

ROBERT LOUIS STEVENSON

Reiki is a useful healing technique to use during our busy lives, whether at home, while traveling, or at work.

Preparing for the Day
How to use Reiki effectively to get ready for a busy day.

Traveling to Work
Harnessing the protective powers of Reiki when you are going to work.

De-stressing at Work
What to do when things go awry in the work place.

Helping Memory and Concentration
Using Reiki at times when you need a little extra focus.

Staying Calm
How to use Reiki to maintain your cool during the busy working day.

Reiki to Ease Tension and Add Energy
Exercises you can try to tackle tension and give you a boost.

Daily Challenge Exercises
How to deal with unexpected occurrences during the day.

Putting the Day to One Side
Relaxing with Reiki.

Worries at the End of the Day
How to get rid of niggling worries.

Getting to Sleep
Simple Reiki tips to help you drift off to sleep easily.

Preparing for the Day

Every day is a new beginning. The refreshing sleep of the night lets your mind and body recover from the previous day and prepare for the new morning, helping you to get ready for whatever life may bring today.

It's useful to start each morning with a quiet time of contemplation. You can do this in different ways—meditate, say a prayer, do energizing exercises—the list is endless. Whatever method you choose, take a few moments to look about you and see the quality of the morning light on a fresh new world. Appreciate your revived, awakening body after its rest and your more positive outlook on life this morning.

You can use Reiki to cleanse your own space. If you are a trained Reiki practitioner, use the power symbol, but otherwise just focus on spreading Reiki energy over the whole area. Alternatively, use a noise, such as a ringing bell, or burn some incense.

Balancing Your Chakras

Before you even get out of bed, try this chakra-balancing exercise to put your whole self back into equilibrium. It's a great way to highlight any problem areas you may have. If your sleep was restless, this simple exercise will enable you to put the night behind you, and move on into the day with a positive approach. Rest in each position until you feel that there is a calming balance and the same amount of energy coming from each chakra (see also page 119). Each stage can take up to about five minutes.

- Lie on your back with your legs touching.
- Place one hand over your forehead (sixth chakra) and the other over the pubic bone (first chakra).
- Remain like this for a few minutes to allow the energy to balance in both places. Your energy will calm and you'll start to feel full of vitality to start the day.
- Now put one hand over the throat area (fifth chakra) and the other over your belly (second chakra) to balance your emotions and allow you to bring out your personal creativity.
- Then put one hand on the fourth chakra in the middle of your chest, and the other on the third chakra on the solar plexus. This position will connect you with your inner strength, so that you can carry out all your actions with integrity and compassion.
- Move one of your hands to the location of the second chakra at your navel and the other on to your forehead at the sixth chakra. This combination brings you deep tranquillity so that you can see everything with a clear head and acknowledge all that is.
- To finish off the exercise, stretch your body and return to the present before you get out of bed.

Out of Bed

Once you are out of bed, but not yet dressed, you could try the following lively exercise, which will bring you into the present moment and let you "lose your mind" in a safe way. You'll feel sharper and ready to take on the day to come—it's a bit like giving your mind a quick shower.

- Sit in comfort, perhaps with your legs crossed, and close your eyes.
- When you are ready just blurt out whatever comes into your head, in stream-of-consciousness style. This need not even be in a recognizable language. Just go with the flow and accept whatever comes out of you.
- If you feel inclined, stand up and dance spontaneously, letting your body do whatever it feels like. Twist and turn, this way and that.
- Now rest, flat on the floor, for a few minutes.
- Return to normal consciousness—ready to seize the day.

Opposite Balance your chakras, then take some lively exercise, to get the day off to a great start.

171

Traveling to Work

If you travel to work every day, you may already have found ways to make it more pleasant and easier to cope with. Perhaps you listen to calming music in your car, or you read a book on your train journey, or spend the time making a to-do list for the day—but have you ever tried Reiki?

Traffic jams, crowds, waiting in queues, and worries about being late are a sure-fire way to make you feel tense before you've even opened up your inbox. However, if you take a few minutes to try out some of the Reiki exercises suggested here, you may find that your working day starts off in a much more positive way.

Long Journeys

Long-distance trips come with their own set of challenges—perhaps you'll have to change time zones and deal with jet lag, find your way around a strange place, adapt to different temperatures and deal with everything in an unfamiliar language. Reiki can help you with these problems, too. Why not give it a try?

Sitting Reiki

If you are sitting down, you can carry out a few subtle Reiki moves—no one need be aware of what you are doing. If you are noticed, it looks as though you are meditating, and there is really nothing odd about that.

- Place your hands just below your collarbones. This will boost your immune system in crowded places.
- To increase your inner confidence, place both hands just above your waist.
- Then move your hands to your waistline—this will release any anxieties you may have.
- Cradle your neck on either side with your hands, your wrists touching. This will strengthen your metabolism.

Self-Protection

It is all too easy to feel unsafe when you are traveling. You may find you are overly conscious of others, or you think they are of you—perhaps not always in a positive way. You may experience a sense of your space being invaded as people push against you or stand too close—though they are probably unable to help it. You may sense a difficult atmosphere, for some reason, and this is likely if there is heavy overcrowding or delays to timetables. It is vital to remain calm and centered in such a situation. We are constantly affected by others, as they are by us—so the more we can hold onto our center the better it will be. If we feel balanced in ourselves, then we can let that feeling disperse to others. The effect will be "catching" and will influence their behavior.

Above Make your daily commute a positive part of your day by using Reiki to keep you relaxed and calm.

Arrival Grounding

The perfect time to practice grounding is if you have traveled to a new place, have arrived, and are getting used to your unfamiliar surroundings. It will help you to center yourself in preparation for what you do next—it will help balance your chakras and bring you strength and peace. You will need privacy to do this, so it is ideal for hotel rooms.

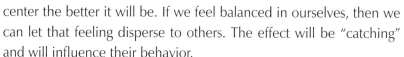

- Stand with your feet a hip-width apart and have your eyes closed, your arms by your sides with palms facing forward.
- Breathe in and out, releasing tension in your shoulders bit by bit.
- Think about your feet, focusing all your attention on them.
- Imagine earth energy coming up to you through your feet and into your left leg.
- Think of the energy entering the first chakra—let it relax.
- Now imagine the energy going down your right leg and back into the earth.
- Now do the same for all seven chakras, one by one.

173

De-stressing at Work

Work, when it's going well, can be great—you feel as though you are "in the zone" and your creative juices are flowing. But at other times the going gets a little tough and you will need to call on extra help to get you through the day.

Above Don't allow unexpected problems at work to push you off course—use Reiki to keep you centered.

Co-workers can be awkward, deadlines may be tight and If you deal with the public, you the strain of being polite and gracious all day, every day, can sometimes be just too much. This is where Reiki can come to your assistance.

A Little Privacy

You may find that some Reiki exercises can be done at your desk without calling undue attention to yourself, while others are just too obvious to be done in a public place. Don't worry—just do the ones you can on the spot and save the rest for when you get home. You may find that it helps to cleanse your desk area by drawing the Reiki power symbol (if you have the required Reiki training to do this) or perhaps breaking up static energy by clapping your hands or ringing a bell. You may even want to burn some cleansing incense. If you work alongside others, some of these suggestions may be inappropriate or even antisocial, so be sensitive to your co workers and use your judgment.

De-stress at Your Desk

You may be coping fine, but sometimes something unexpected comes along that seems to throw you off course—an angry phone call, a sharply worded email, or an uncalled-for comment. You may feel undermined and put-upon. Now's the time to do a quick de-stressing treatment to get yourself back to normal, regain your confidence, and carry on performing at your best. Hold each Reiki position for a few minutes before moving on to the next one.

- Sitting in your usual chair, breathe in and out deeply several times, watching your breath. Release all your stress with each out-breath.
- Now cradle the back of your head with one hand and hold your forehead with the other. You'll find that your thoughts will calm down and that the tension you've been holding will drift away.
- Place one hand on your stomach and the other on your forehead. You'll start to feel more centered and in control.
- Let one hand remain on your stomach, but let the other move to your chest. You'll find that this has a balancing effect.

If you have felt a bad mood coming on at work, this exercise can help to lift it. Just do it in the same way, but focus on your mood rather than on your stress.

Protecting the Aura with Reiki

One way to protect the Self from harm is to use your personal aura. This can help you feel strong and supported, enabling you to feel calm and safe from negative influences. Here is an easy Reiki meditation you can try on yourself, and it is very effective if you feel you need to protect yourself. You can do it before entering a threatening place or intimidating atmosphere. If you are treating another person, you can do this visualization for both of you.

- Sit down comfortably and think of your aura being filled with your own Reiki energy.
- Think of the outer edge of the aura being a hard shell, which cannot be pierced by damaging forces, holding your Reiki energy around you and in you.
- Imagine the Reiki energy emanating from your hands and filling up the whole of this space, protecting and cleansing you.

Helping Memory and Concentration

Perhaps you have to take an exam or give a presentation, and need to rely on your memory and composure to get you through. On top of your own nervousness, your environment may distract you.

Concentrating to order can be a problem for some people. But Reiki can help you gather your strength and prepare you for the task ahead. The following exercise will calm your nerves, assist your focus, help you to feel less stressed, and stop your mind racing nervously.

Heightening your Concentration

Find a Reiki partner (a Reiki practitioner) to treat you while you relax. If possible, find a suitable place to lie down. This will enable you to de-stress more completely.

• As the giver, place your hands over the receiver's eyes and forehead. Let your palms rest on their cheeks. This will allow their eyes to rest and energy to move into their body.

• Put your hands on the receiver's head, with your fingertips on their temples on each side, above their ears.

• Cradle the receiver's head in your hands with the fingertips over their medulla oblongata. They will start to feel more balanced in the left and right brain and be able to memorize things better.

Disturbed Memory

Memory is all about absorbing, storing, and then recalling information to order, using your short- and long-term memory. How well you can retrieve information depends on how well you have been able to store it in your long-term memory. Although it is impossible to reverse permanent loss of memory, there are plenty of things you can do to keep your memory functioning well.

176

Reiki Self-Treatments to Help Memory

You can carry out this sequence on yourself very easily—whenever you need to improve your powers of memory.

- Position your hands over your eyes, with the palms just resting on your cheeks.
- Now put both hands on your head, with your palms on your temples and your fingers pointing toward your crown. You can balance the two sides of your brain like this, improving your memory.
- Position your hands on either side of your head with your ears covered.
- Put your hands around the back of your head on either side and cradle it.
- Now place your hands around your neck with your wrists in contact in the middle.

Above Boost your memory to improve your performance in an exam or during a presentation.

A Reiki Shower for Added Focus

When you need to bring yourself to the center and focus your thoughts, try giving yourself a Reiki shower. This involves absorbing Reiki energy and it is great for concentrating on a specific task.

- Relax in your chair and close your eyes. Breathe slowly and deeply and observe your breath going in and out.
- Place your hands in the classic "prayer" position, palms and fingers together pointing upward, at your chest level.
- Now lift both arms above your head, keeping them apart.
- Turning the palms downward, bring them down so that they are just above the top of your head.
- Feel the "shower" of Reiki coming from your palms, flowing through your whole body, dispersing negativity all the way down.
- Draw your hands, with palms facing toward you, up and down in front of your body.
- Lastly, let your palms face the floor to let the negative energy move out and down. Return your hands to the prayer position.
- Give thanks to the cosmos for the Reiki energy you have received. Repeat this exercise several times until you feel fully replenished.

177

Staying Calm

Stress is a normal part of life, but it can be very unwelcome. However, it may be useful to remember that stress can help us to carry out tasks and face up to difficult situations far better than we might do otherwise.

Above: Staying clam will help you perform better in stressful situations.

Our inbuilt "fight or flight" response is designed to help us cope with emergencies—it once helped us survive under threat of attack, for example. So stress is a useful, practical energy that it is vital to harness when we are using our creative side.

In our modern life, you probably notice that difficult life events are usually experienced as being extremely stressful: bereavement, divorce, moving house, and other momentous changes, where you really do have to make big adjustments. Remaining calm will help you to get through many challenging predicaments during the day, and help you perform tasks better. It is key to being able to exercise your skills effectively and get on with other people well.

When feeling stressed becomes unmanageable and a threat to your health, stopping you achieving things and dealing with life well, then you need to take steps to calm down. On the practical side, it's a good idea to avoid consuming caffeine, animal proteins and fats. Good, regular exercise out of doors and participating in competitive sports are also both excellent ways of calming the nerves.

If you feel you are losing your cool at any point, try a little calming Reiki to put you back on track. Perhaps you are plagued by constant interruptions when you are trying to complete a task, or people keep distracting you with casual conversation, or your phone keeps ringing. If possible, keep up an appearance of being cool at all times. That way you will start to feel cool within yourself, too.

Cleanse your Reiki practice area, whether this is your bedroom or a special meditation or Reiki treatment room, by carrying out your favorite cleansing ritual. This will help you focus on the task ahead. To do this use sound, such as clapping your hands or ringing a singing bowl or bell, or chant, or burn a smudge stick or incense of your choice to do this.

Keeping Cool

This exercise is particularly effective when you are starting up new ventures and need to feel sure of yourself.

- Place your hands across your upper chest, with the fingers butting up against each other. This position can help you turn around negativity.
- Now put your hands across your rib cage so that the fingers touch each other. This allows you to trust more easily.
- Move your hands horizontally to your waist area and let your fingers touch. You will feel more balanced and less fearful.
- Now put your hands on your back, at waist height, with the fingers touching each other on your spine. You will start to feel more confident and calm.

Calming Reiki Meditation

Use this simple meditation technique to help you feel connected to the divine and to yourself, too. Use it to allow you to go within— further and further. As a daily practice you will find that you can calm your mind and focus on the still space inside. Giving Reiki energy to yourself helps connect you with the spirit.

- Sit down on a small pillow and close your eyes. You can cross your legs if this is comfortable for you.
- Breathe naturally in and out and watch your breath. Notice it slowing down, moving in and out.
- Place your hands in your opposite armpits, and direct your focus to the space in between them.
- Feel the connectedness within you, and your connection with the world and the universe.

179

Reiki to Ease Tension and Add Energy

When you are working in a concentrated way, you may feel full of energy and confidence, but then suddenly experience a dip and feel a need to have a break and regroup—to gather your thoughts.

Sometimes you'll need to ease physical tension, too—especially if it gathers in the shoulder area. If you have been sitting in one position, say at a computer, this may be particularly relevant. Reiki can help give you a quick boost whenever you need extra energy in your system, and it is a very useful and immediate way of reviving yourself.

Easing Shoulder Tension

Try out this simple self-help Reiki position. It's especially useful if you have a desk job and are sitting still for long hours.

- Position your hands over your shoulders, with the fingertips facing over them toward your back. This will ease any aches and pains in your back and help you to relax generally.
- If you experience an energy lapse during the afternoon after lunch, lay your hands on your stomach, one above the other. This will help sustain you through the rest of the day.
- Now stand up and place both hands on your lower back in a V-shape. You'll find that it helps you feel more sure of yourself and better able to deal with any new difficulties.
- Sit down again and place both hands across your stomach, fingers pointing toward each other. This position will enable you to release all annoyances and balance your energies.

Quick-Fix Boost

Spend just a few minutes trying this easy exercise to boost your energy and you will reap the rewards. If you are working in an office, and cannot lie down, try it sitting in your usual chair. But if you work from home, you'll find lying down is more relaxing.

- Lie down on a soft rug or mat and close your eyes. Relax.
- Place both hands, one above the other, over your solar plexus and stomach areas. Keep your fingers as relaxed as possible.
- Let your mind drift off. Remain like this for up to fifteen minutes and you will feel refreshed afterwards.

Energy Reinforcement

Try this quick and easy Reiki exercise when you need to pep up your energy levels. Hold each position for a few minutes.

- Put one hand on your eyes and the other across the back of your head, so that your whole head feels cupped between your hands.
- Now move your hands to your chest, place one in the center, and then the other on your throat.
- Put one hand on your stomach, around the navel area and the other above it at solar plexus level.
- Lay one hand on your seventh chakra and the other gently over your first chakra.

Above: Find the energy you need, using Reiki positions, to help you through difficult meetings.

Giving Yourself More Confidence

There are times during any busy day when you just need a little lift. Use this simple Reiki exercise to focus your energies and give you the boost you need to carry out your tasks efficiently. You'll find that it helps you adjust and be able to adapt to what you need to do quickly.

- Sitting in your chair, place your hands on your upper chest, fingertips meeting in the center. This will help you turn your thoughts around and, if they are in a negative place, you will start to feel more positive.
- Now move your hands to your ribs, again letting your fingertips meet. This will help you face up to new predicaments.
- Shift your hands lower down, to your waistline, letting your fingertips contact one another. Your confidence will start to rise.
- Move your hands to your back waist, fingers meeting in the center, on your spine.

181

Daily Challenge Exercises

No matter how calmly you approach all that happens during your day, sometimes something will come out of left field and threaten to derail your confidence. Simple Reiki exercises can come to your assistance, helping to carry you through with ease.

Above: Combat a sudden lack of confidence using Reiki.

Getting Ready for an Important Client

Perhaps a straightforward-seeming meeting is in the diary, but all of a sudden you feel daunted by it and experience your confidence ebbing away. If this occurs, try the following reassuring Reiki exercise to restore you, helping you feel you can do a great job.

• Sit in your chair with your eyes closed. Keep your shoulders relaxed and place your hands loosely on your legs. Breathe steadily in and out and, as you breathe out, sigh a little.

• Place your hands in your armpits and focus attention on the heart center in between—you'll soon feel calm again.

• Now place your hands over your eyes, with palms resting on your cheeks.

• Move your hands to your chest to bring both sides of your body into harmony.

• Put one hand above the other, horizontally, on your stomach. Feel grounded and supported in all you do.

Thinking Clearly and Calming Nervousness

Perhaps you have to prepare yourself for a stage performance or to make a speech, or perhaps present some new ideas coherently. This calls you to make a real effort to project well, so that all your skills and preparation are displayed impressively. You need to show yourself off at your very best and this is your big chance. You may be experiencing stage fright and feel that you will not be able to give your best, or you may notice physical reactions of clammy palms, nervous shaking or sweating. However, there are Reiki exercises you can do to calm yourself down and prepare for the big moment.

• Put your hands on either side of your head, with your palms toward your face. They need to be just above your ears. This will harmonize you and bring your right- and left-brain facilities together. You will be able to think through complex issues in a relaxed way.

- Now put your hands on the back of your head, cradling it gently. You will feel supported in your fears and rational thoughts.
- Finally, put one hand over your third chakra (see page 119) and the other on your forehead on your sixth chakra. This will calm your wobbly stomach and any jittery feelings. You will be able to stop "fearing the worst'.
- Now return to the present and carry out your task with aplomb.

Self-Protection

Sometimes you need to protect yourself from difficult people. Some people are harder to get along with than others, particularly in the work environment—perhaps they want their own ideas to go forward and they don't listen to others. Reiki can assist you in dealing with this. With a little Reiki help, you can put your thoughts and feelings into perspective and face such individuals with calm confidence.

- Raise your arms into a "tent" shape over the top of your head and close your eyes.
- Imagine yourself as sitting inside a tent. No one can touch you or harm you. You are protected. Reiki energy is being concentrated inside your tent, guarding you and giving you strength.

You can also make a Reiki self-protection bubble for yourself. This will help you to deal with difficult people more easily and deflect their negative energy.

- Sit quietly with your eyes closed. Remain alert.
- Visualize a light in front of you and focus on it.
- Imagine the light moving toward you, gradually enveloping you— feel as though you are sitting inside your own protective bubble.
- Now imagine the outside of the bubble becoming strong, like an impenetrable shell.
- Visualize the light inside the shell washing over and through you.
- Think about the light protecting you from harmful influences and remaining with you forever.
- Stay with this vision for a few minutes.
- Breathe deeply—then let the vision drift away and open your eyes again.

Putting the Day to One Side

When you've had a busy day or a hectic week, it is sometimes very difficult to switch off and stop dwelling on all the things that took place. This makes it all the harder to put those thoughts to one side, relax, and turn you attention to leisure pursuits.

I f your day went well, you may keep replaying the good moments, to relive the positive feelings you had at the time. If things went badly, perhaps you feel that you could have handled them better and negative thoughts keep tormenting you. Perhaps you need a change of pace after a busy day to clear your mind. Reiki can help you calm down and feel more relaxed, helping you to benefit from your downtime. Some people find that it helps to put their feet up with a hot drink, have a refreshing soak in a bath, and change into casual clothes. Others find cooking a meal creative and relaxing. The following Reiki exercise can help you shift into a different mode and mind-set—preparing you for a relaxing interlude. Spend a few moments centering yourself and letting your whole body relax completely.

• Lie on the floor, on a soft rug or mat, with a comfy pillow under your head. Breathe in and out deeply, and each time you breathe out, imagine yourself sinking deeper into the floor.

• Place your hands on your eyes, palms on your cheeks. This pose offers you balance and calm. It can help you address what you are "seeing" in your daily life, and what you are not facing up to or are avoiding.

• Move your hands to your head, on either side, with your fingers pointing upward. You'll find that your thoughts settle and focus.

• Now cradle the back of your head in both hands. This pose calms and steadies you. If you have worries, they will drift away.

• Place your hands on your chest, with your fingertips just meeting in the center. The negative thoughts you've been holding onto will gradually fade with each breath, until you don't notice them any more.

- Move your hands to your waistline to bring energy back to you and dissipate any residual feelings of panic and stress.
- Finally, sit up on your cushion and place your hands on your back, at waist height. Your fingers need to meet in the center of your back. Your well-being and get-up-and-go will soon return to you.

Self-Relaxation with Reiki

If you can't stop your mind racing—it may be jumping from one thought to another—you need to find a way of calming and focusing. This Reiki exercise is very simple to carry out, and will help you wind down even further. It will relax both body and mind and bring them into harmony.

- Lie down on a soft surface such as a rug or a mat, with a soft pillow beneath your head. Let your hands flop open, palms facing upward, by your sides.
- Watch your breath flow in and out, noticing it slowing down. Breathe in through your nose and out through your mouth. Allow yourself to sigh out loud each time you breathe out, so that you can release even more tension.
- Focus attention on your feet, calves, knees, thighs, and hips in turn. At each location let all the stress go.
- Move gradually upward through your body, focusing on each place in turn, and letting the tension go each time.

Left: Make sure you can switch off from work in order to enjoy relaxing leisure pursuits.

185

Worries at the End of the Day

Worry, anxiety, and depression can be very destructive. Worry can eat away at your mind and spoil whatever else you are trying to think about or achieve, added to which, it's an activity that is wasteful of your energy. Depression, if untreated, can take over your life.

Above: Don't allow worry and anxiety to take over your life.

Anxiety is when you feel more aware than normal of being fearful about something, and this can feel debilitating, to such an extent that life seems overwhelming. However, a certain amount of stress can be a good thing in life—it gets us moving forward and helps us to deal with tricky situations and emergencies.

Quite often worries and mild depression reflect fears about what we imagine might happen, and often there is no logic behind these thoughts—they often get to us when we are at our most tired and vulnerable.

As a first option, you could try avoiding those foods that make you feel "jittery", such as caffeine and sugars, and you'll find that taking plenty of exercise helps your mind to calm down.

Releasing Your Worries

Whenever you need to release worry, or escape from a pattern of worrying, try to get back in touch with "now" and let your worrying thoughts drift away with this helpful Reiki practice.

• Sit quietly in a chair and place your hands over your eyes, with your palms resting on your cheeks.

186

- Move your hands to your head—cupping it on either side and allowing your fingertips to meet at the top. This will relax you and help you to think clearly.
- Now hold the back of your head in the same way—to relax the mind and calm you down. You will feel more secure in every way.
- Put your hands on either side of your chest, with your fingertips meeting in the middle. This will help release any negativity you have been experiencing and boost feelings of positivity.
- Finally, put your hands, pointing downward, on your lower back. You'll start to feel more confident and less stressed.

Reiki to Help Depression

There are many levels of depression, spanning a range from mild but temporary sadness to severe hopelessness, indicating psychiatric illness. Causes may be biological or psychological. You may find it helpful to keep a daily journal of spontaneous writing to "write out" your deepest thoughts, or try out positive visualization meditations. When practicing Reiki, you'll find it most useful to focus on your head, your heart, and your solar plexus.

Depression can be a very debilitating condition, getting to us when we least expect it. If you feel that your condition is more than just a temporary "down" patch, you need to see your doctor in the first instance.

If your depression seems to be mild and temporary and a response to your circumstances, try to give yourself some gentle healing treatment. This Reiki exercise eases symptoms and allows you to reconnect with your upbeat side once more.

- Sit in a comfortable chair and place your hands on your head, with your fingertips meeting over the top.
- Now cup the back of your head with both hands, fingertips meeting.
- Place both hands on your chest, below your collarbone, and let the middle fingers come into contact.
- Move your hands to your waistline and allow your fingertips to touch in the center.
- Now stand up and put your hands behind you, holding your waist.

187

Getting to Sleep

Dropping off quickly to sleep at your regular bedtime and remaining asleep all night can be difficult. It may even be unrealistic—especially if your day has been unusually hectic and your brain is finding it hard to "switch off". If you know you have to be up bright and early the next day, this can put added pressure on you to get a full night's sleep. This very thought can prevent you from falling asleep.

I f you are running through a number of different issues in your mind, use the time to solve some of the less serious ones—this may calm you and let you fall asleep. For example, you may be planning what to wear the next day—make your decisions now and then move on to another solvable problem. This could be planning your journey to an appointment, deciding when to leave home, or decide what to cook in the evening. Once you have resolved these issues, you can move on.

It's a good idea to go through some pre-sleep exercises to prepare fully for the night. That way you can feel calm in mind, body, and spirit, with all your chakras in harmony. If you happen to fall asleep mid-exercise this is all to the good—Reiki has worked for you. Remain in the same positions for up to five minutes to receive maximum benefit.

- Lie on your back and make yourself as comfortable as possible. Position your hands over your eyes, with your palms resting lightly on your cheeks.
- Now move your hands to your chest over your fourth chakra (see page 119).
- Change position so that one hand rests on your solar plexus and the other is just below it, on your waistline. You will relax deeply now.
- Position both hands in a V-formation over your pubic area—fingertips in contact.

When you are lying in bed, why not try this simple Reiki treatment to calm your mind and body? It encourages the relaxation you need to drop off easily and quickly. If you wake in the night,

after having been asleep, try it again to help you get back to sleep.
- Lie either on your back or your side—whichever feels most natural and comfortable.
- Place one hand over your forehead and the other on your belly and simply watch your regular breathing pattern, noticing how your belly rises and falls in time with it.
- Remain like this for about ten minutes—you may find that you actually fall asleep in this position.

Waking in the Night

If you wake in the middle of the night, or you wake up too early in the morning, try out this easy exercise to return you to sleep. The action of watching your breath should have the effect of distracting your mind from dwelling on thoughts that could keep you awake.

- Lying flat on your back in bed, place your hands on your stomach, with your fingertips in contact. Focus on the rising and falling of your breath under your hands. Watch your breath going in and out and keep your attention on this.
- Move your hands to your solar plexus and let your fingertips touch. Carry on watching your breath.
- Put your hands on your chest, one above the other. Concentrate on your breath going in and out.
- Finally, lay one hand on your forehead and the other below your navel. Carry on watching your breath.

Left: It is important to get a good night's sleep. Reiki can help you to relax.

Chapter 8
Living With Reiki

> *"To see a world*
> *in a grain of sand*
> *And a heaven*
> *in a wild flower*
> *Hold infinity in*
> *the palm*
> *of your hand*
> *And eternity in*
> *an hour"*

WILLIAM BLAKE

Living With Reiki
How to bring Reiki into every part of your life.

Protection
Using Reiki to protect ourselves from opposing influences in the outside world.

Closing Down After Healing
Procedures to disengage yourself emotionally after working with another person. These are necessary for self-protection.

Reiki and other Physical Therapies
Used in conjunction with other therapies, Reiki can increase its healing power still further.

Kirlian Photography Healing Test
Demonstrates graphically the effect of Reiki on a receiver's energy field.

The Origins of Reiki
Biographies of the first three practitioners of the system.

The Five Spiritual Principles of Reiki
Reiki's basic principles, forming guidelines for a healthy life, both emotionally and physically.

Living With Reiki

To live with Reiki is living with awareness. Whether it is in our home, with our friends, the food we eat, or the work we do: if we carry the awareness of Reiki with us, it will bring an element of love to our day-to-day lives. Hawayo Takata once said: "Reiki is unconditional love: when given from one person to another sometimes miracles occur." This is also true of everything we come into contact with. If we treat all those that we meet with respect they will, in turn, respect us. And as we develop compassion for ourselves we find we have more compassion for others.

Applying the Reiki principles on page 166 enhances our ability to flow with the ups and downs of life. If we can pull back from our attachment to a set course of action or outcome, and simply allow things to evolve, then we are less likely to become stressed. Everything that happens can then be seen as part of our life adventure.

Reiki in the Home

Everyone has walked into a house and felt its atmosphere. This feeling is made up of the issues and experiences of all who live in or visit that house. If someone holds a strong emotional issue in their field, the home they live in will also contain the essence of that issue.

So our homes are an expression of who we are. If we wish them to reflect the serenity we have found on an inner

"Home is where the heart is."

level, we can use Reiki to do this. Every task we choose to do will carry energy if it is done with awareness of the Reiki energy. Simple tasks, such as doing the dishes, take on a new perspective when we choose to do them with love.

In addition, you can clean each room in your house by invoking the energy and intending it to transform all low vibratory energy within the room. Use the second degree symbols, if you know them, to seal the corners as described on page 88-93, and apply the same techniques to your home as you would to your healing room.

Facing page
Your home reflects who you are. It is a canvas on which you can allow your creativity to express itself.

Left When you carry out everyday household jobs, do them with love.

Reiki With Children

A child is our teacher and it is best that we remember this fact. For children the veil of forgetfulness is not yet formed—they can still remember where they have just come from. It is a delicate balance to teach a child the ways of the world and yet help them retain the freedom and innocence of youth for as long as possible.

When asked if Reiki is suitable for children I often reply that children are Reiki. They are the most vital bundles of energetic love and joy you can find on this planet. If ever I begin to feel the world is a dark place and my heart is heavy, I make a point of watching children to remind myself of the simple joys of living. Only a child can shout in pure ecstasy at simply being alive.

To treat a child with Reiki can prove difficult, simply because children cannot sit still, and they become bored very easily. Better to wait for them to come to you. Unfortunately, this means that they will probably be crying about their grazed knee or cut finger. But most children are resilient by nature and often just need a little rub

Below Reiki can add great healing energy to parental comforting and enhance the closeness of the relationship.

or kiss from mom before they are off again shouting and yelling. In these cases Reiki is an excellent option as it works by simply placing your hand on the area that hurts.

Reiki also comes into its own at bedtime, as children will be more receptive to you connecting with them. You may tell stories or sing to them as you give Reiki.

In the case of more serious illnesses Reiki can, of course, be used alongside any other medication or therapies being administered. In these instances, you may find the time needed to treat children is greatly reduced.

Above Children remind us of spontaneity, freedom, and joy. Within our hearts we are all children.

"*I would be a sad man if it were not for the hope I see in my grandchild's eyes.*"

CHIEF DAN GEORGE

Below

All animals on this planet are our teachers, showing us our connection to the Great Mystery and the intelligence of living in harmony with our environment.

Reiki With Animals

Animals, like humans, thrive on touch, and they respond to Reiki in the same way that a human being does. There are many people experimenting with Reiki in livestock farming—I have heard of farms in Australia that use Reiki on cattle, and seen people using Reiki to calm horses. I have treated many dogs and cats myself—some that healed at an incredible rate as a result.

Animals seem to have a problem sitting still and may, at first, find Reiki an unusual experience. However, once they have received it a few times they will become far more receptive. You will probably find that they start coming to you for regular treatments.

Reiki and Food

Remember: it is not only food that we ingest. Each day we feed off a mountain of junk from television, newspaper headlines, politics, advertising, the air we breathe, the water we drink, the thought forms we hear, and so on. It is, therefore, important to pay particular attention to what you take on board your bodily vessel, in both mind and body.

Reiki can have a positive role to play in this aspect of our lives. Through the awareness we gain we can take more responsibility for what we ingest. Once you have awareness of ki, the difference in vibration between a microwaved hamburger and a lovingly prepared meal with fresh vegetables—if not already obvious—will become startlingly so. The relative benefits of ingesting either one will also be fairly apparent. The choice then is yours. The same goes for what you choose to watch on television, read in newspapers, and forms of information and entertainment.

Reiki can also benefit us in our preparation of food. If you imagine that a constant stream of energy is now flowing through you from the universal supply of ki, then everything you touch turns to gold. As you prepare a meal the food will be infused with life-giving ki.

"It's not the food that keeps you going, it's the chi in the food."

THE BAREFOOT DOCTOR

Right The plants in your garden will benefit from Reiki— helping to nourish them as they grow.

Plants and Reiki in Your Home

We can benefit the plants in our home or garden with Reiki and there are some very simple ways to do this. Carry the awareness of Reiki as you walk around the plants, pruning and watering them. Take time to let the energy flow and send them love. Before watering the plants hold the watering can or hose in your hands for a few minutes and simply give it Reiki. Allow the ki to infuse the water so that it contains more nourishment for the plants. When planting, give Reiki to the roots of the plant before putting it into the ground.

Reiki With Plants

Plants operate in the same field of energy as we do, so they also benefit from receiving ki to stimulate and nourish them. Plants seem to respond positively to human touch and attention, and when this touch is imbued with the universal ki, the benefits received are multiplied.

I remember a story I was told about an oak tree that stood beside the path to a meditation sanctuary. It had been planted at the same time as all the other oaks in the garden, but this one was appreciated on a daily basis. As all the members of the community walked past it on their way to meditation they would remark, "Oh what a lovely oak tree". As a result it had grown at a much faster rate than the others in the garden and appeared more bushy and healthy. It shows us that as we appreciate things they respond and grow stronger and more beautiful.

"The complexity of New York City is to a square mile of lowland tropical rain forest as a mouse's squeak is to all the music that has ever been produced by humanity."

DANIEL JANZEN

199

Above Reiki can be stimulating for people in their later years, and may open up whole new areas of their consciousness.

Reiki With the Elderly

Older people often become lonely and isolated in today's society, the world and its people moving too quickly to listen to them. Many older people have lost friends, family, or their own partner. Even if they have people to talk to they may well often be deprived of physical touch. Contact with other humans or animals can be deeply nurturing—if we are deprived of it we can feel unloved and emotionally unsupported. This need is acute in some elderly people, especially if they are unable to look after a pet or do not benefit from regular close interaction with others.

There are, however, problems that present themselves in treating the elderly. It is difficult to employ techniques such as massage, for example, because of physical frailty or personal inhibitions so Reiki offers a nonintrusive therapy that can be carried out in most environments. And because it re-energizes areas of the body that may be under-exercised, such as stiff or arthritic joints, it can bring enormous benefits and improved quality of life.

Reiki can be used safely with most other medication (see contraindications on page 207) and therefore presents no problems to any care the elderly person may already be receiving. In addition, a person is never too old to change their beliefs about life, and the use of Reiki may present the challenges that stimulate new levels of consciousness. I encourage elderly people to take the first degree Reiki course, as I have seen it bring renewed vigor. Young or old, most of us just want to be useful in some way, and age does not affect the body's ability to channel Reiki.

Reiki With the Dying

Death is such a mystery; we know so little about it. Many teachings tell us that it is merely the letting go of your dream self, your physical body, and other self-containing layers of your mortal personality. The destination is a place you are already in—you never left. Christ talked about the veil of forgetfulness to describe living in mortal flesh. This veil is in place to ensure we buy into the illusion of who we think we are. Once the veil is removed at the time of death we remember who we were all along. So the more we identify with our mortal flesh, the harder that transition may be. It could be that we spend our whole lives believing that God doesn't exist, and is merely the deluded imaginings of dreamers, only to find out that God does exist and existed within us all this time. For this reason, I believe it is important to keep an open mind.

People who develop their awareness through life, particularly through practices such as meditation, are simply working to remove the veil of forgetfulness while still clothed in mortal flesh. At times they may experience breakthroughs in their meditations where they feel the intimate union with all that is. Similarly, people practicing Reiki experience this union on a regular basis, as they are intimately connected to the universal ki. In addition, many Reiki practitioners report feeling, or seeing, the presence of angelic beings around them when they are working.

For this reason Reiki can have great benefits for those people who are near to this transition themselves. It provides a supportive energy and a quality of experience that is very similar to what they will experience as they move out of denser realms into more vibratory ones. Reiki can help people let go of their attachment to the physical, as it brings them closer to the higher vibratory realms.

When asked to treat people who are terminally ill, remind them that Reiki will assist them in whichever way they need it most. It may simply help them to move on from this physical experience to the next stage of their infinite adventure.

It is important not to confuse healing with providing a cure. Sometimes the healing may be a shift of awareness that allows a person to open up to their feelings and make peace in their lives before moving on. In the event that death was sudden and unexpected, the second degree symbols can be used to send healing to the person after they have left the body, to assist them in overcoming the shock.

> *"A little while, a moment of rest upon the wind and another woman shall bear me."*
>
> KAHLIL GIBRAN

201

Protection

This is a subject that is often talked about by people who are in the process of self development. As we become more sensitive to the subtle energies in the world, we also become more aware of the stronger energies. It is not that we suddenly become vulnerable to the world and the people in it; rather that we become aware of the world, the people in it, and the effects our interactions have on us.

I often find that after the first degree course people open up to universal love and leave the workshop feeling safe and amazed at their own capacity to feel shifts in energy around others, as well as changes in their own fields. Then on Monday morning they head off into work full of enthusiasm, but instead of experiencing universal love they meet resistance in the fields of everyone at work, and sense all the fear, suffering, and unresolved conflicts that these people carry.

The Stone and the Flower

The spiritual teacher and Zen Master Osho once described this experience as the difference in awareness between a stone and a flower. The stone, though alive, is dense and asleep. It has great resilience to the effects of the elements around it. The flower, on the other hand, is vibrant and awake, radiating colors and perfumes into the world. It seems so much more alive than the stone, but is vulnerable to the elements and easily damaged. As we become more aware, we make the transition from stone to flower. We become more vibrant and colorful. We also become more sensitive to the world around us. We might start to feel other people's pain in our own bodies and, for example, we may feel exhausted from a simple trip to the city center.

So as we become more aware of ourselves, and get to know what our personal energy

Below The stone and the flower represent our different forms of awareness.

feels like, we are far more conscious of the effects that the world and the people in it have on us. This demonstrates the simple truth that our fields change as we release emotional patterns and belief systems. The signature they carry shifts. When we return to familiar situations that previously presented no problems to us, we suddenly can't cope with the experience. It is too painful because we are able to feel the pain that previously we couldn't.

Erecting Barriers

Many people devise all kinds of elaborate ways to protect themselves. These normally involve placing some kind of barrier between themselves and the world. These devices can never be truly effective because their philosophy is ill-conceived.

Above There is no separation other than the separation created in your mind. Every person you meet is an expression of the same being.

Let me explain. You are walking down the street feeling at one with the world. Coming in the other direction is a man feeling incredibly angry with the world, closed off and looking for conflict. You feel his pain and anger. You then erect your wall, but it's too late because you have felt his pain and anger—it is already in you. Any attempt to block it out only serves to block it in. The wall you erected actually traps his feelings within you. As you placed your protection between yourself and his anger and pain, you actually created separation between his experience and your own. You made a judgment of him and decided that you wanted to exclude him from your experience. The oneness you were experiencing previously didn't include him. But of course it does—we are all one. He is a part of you.

Accepting Others

So what do we do? To answer, I will recount an experience that I believe I was given to teach me this principle.

In 1995 I was living in a spiritual community in the north of Scotland, surrounded by supportive and loving people. I had to visit London for a seminar, so found myself on the underground in the center of the city. We pulled into a station and, as the doors opened, I felt a ripple of fear go through me. I noticed that the same ripple went right down the train, affecting everyone on it. The next moment a huge man entered the train. He was drunk, very angry, and looking for someone to challenge him. He came over to where I was sitting, threw the man who was sitting opposite me off the seat, and sat down.

Everyone on the train was trying to shrink into a corner, such was the power of this man's projections. He started to loudly sing songs that were designed to insult everyone on the train.

After his first song he looked at me. I found myself able to hold his gaze, even though I wanted to look away and hide like everyone

Below A simple handshake can dissolve fears and exchange compassion in a threatening world.

else on the train. I noticed that he was enjoying himself. As I looked at him I felt myself accepting him for who he was and empathizing with him. I felt fear but I knew it wasn't mine—it was his fear.

He asked me what I thought of his song. I told him that it was an angry song. He replied: "Of course it was an angry song, I'm an anarchist." He sang another song and looked back at me and, almost as if he realized that I was his friend, he held out his hands—they were covered in scratches and blood—and said he had hurt himself. I took hold of one of his hands and the fear in me dissolved. I was holding the hands of a scared young man who wanted love and attention, not an angry man who might hurt me.

The rest of the journey was uneventful. When his stop arrived he got up, said goodbye, and left. It was only then that I noticed the rest of the people on the train. They were all staring at me as if I had disarmed a man with a machine gun.

When I left the train I felt rushes of ecstasy through my body as the whole experience—all the fear, anger, and sadness—left me. This taught me that if we are prepared to experience others fully, and do not engage in conflict with them, they cannot hurt us and, when we move out of their fields, the experience lifts off us effortlessly.

Being open and developing yourself means that you will feel the pain of those who have not yet made the choice to re-connect to their hearts and feelings. When this pain becomes a burden to you it is important to know that it is a warning. Retreat and take time to re-center and balance yourself.

A Containment Exercise

Before leaving home in the morning, this simple exercise will help you gather yourself. Imagine that a powerful magnet sits just below your navel, which is designed to attract only the energy that belongs to you. Your navel is the switch. Press the switch, turn on the magnet, and visualize all the parts of yourself returning to you from wherever they may be. Once you are complete, imagine a belt of light activating from your base chakra and spinning counter-clockwise around you, passing through each chakra on its way up to your crown. Use the affirmation

"I am the presence activating my electronic belt at the speed of light now". This belt will contain all your energy, and will help you to maintain your center and boundaries.

Closing Down After Healing

Just as we go to great lengths to prepare and open ourselves for healing, so we must also close down again afterward and make sure we disengage from the person we are working with. This serves to close our crown, which will be open after healing, and disengage from our receiver to avoid them becoming dependent on us as healers. This is simply done through a combination of intention and visualization.

As you finish working with your receiver, place your hands on their shoulders if they are sitting, or their feet if they are lying down. Thank your guides for helping you and slowly detach yourself from the person. Now go and wash your hands. As you wash work through the following visualization: imagine that each chakra is a flower. Each flower is the color of the corresponding chakra, red for base, orange for sacral, and so on. Starting with the crown, see the flower as brilliant and open, then close it so that it becomes a bud. Continue through each chakra until they are all closed.

Exercising Caution

There are few contraindications to worry about when giving Reiki. In most cases, following these simple precautions will ensure a safe treatment.

- Always ensure that broken bones are set in a cast before giving Reiki. This is because Reiki's efficiency to heal bones is remarkable in the early stages of a break, and if the bone is not set properly it may heal incorrectly.
- Caution should be taken when treating people with heart problems, especially if they have been fitted with artificial devices such as pacemakers, as Reiki may affect the device itself.
- Pregnant women should always be treated with care, particularly in the early stages of pregnancy. Most alternative therapies advise caution in this situation and Reiki is no exception.
- Care should be taken when treating people with diabetes. Reiki has been shown to affect the levels of insulin required by the body, so simply warn the receiver that they need to monitor their insulin levels closely if they are to receive treatments.
- Always reduce the length of treatments on children. Usually they will become restless when they have had enough.
- Avoid giving Reiki after drinking alcohol.
- Avoid giving Reiki to anyone who is under the influence of alcohol or drugs.

Protect Yourself

- The main awareness you need to carry for protection is the knowledge that you are safe. Think of the sun—it continues to shine, unaffected by the darkness around it.
- Being centered, grounded, and open-hearted can also help when dealing with external conflict.
- Ensure you are grounded. Simply focus your awareness downward and feel the earth supporting you. Open up your base center. Shift your awareness from your solar plexus, where you will be experiencing the conflict, and focus your awareness on your heart center.
- Breathe into your heart and imagine the center expanding and opening. You may feel warmth enter it as you do this.
- Observe the person you want to protect yourself from and remember that any negative behavior is simply a survival response because, at some time, they have not received love. Send love from your heart and simply think "I accept you as you are, you are a part of me."

Reiki and Other Physical Therapies

Jennifer Gresty has been a practitioner for over twenty years, specializing in deep tissue massage. She is a qualified reflexologist and aromatherapist and has taught ITEC therapeutic massage for over fifteen years. This is her experience of Reiki.

"I had been interested in doing a Reiki course for some time, although I really didn't expect it to create a big shift for me, even though I wanted to work on a deeper level. I am astounded by the degree to which Reiki has affected my life, not only in my work but also on a personal level. It brought a lot of deep issues to the surface and has enabled me to pass through emotional crossroads. It has helped me to accept who I am, and empowered me to change aspects of my life. It has helped me value myself. I feel far more grounded and have the desire to meditate more, with more focus in my meditations. I feel more guided in my whole life and, in some way, safer. I have this profound sense of security.

"After the Reiki course I felt like I had been plugged in. My work has been enhanced beyond belief, and I have been able to break through boundaries with certain clients that I would have been unable to do before. When I go into a session now I am far more aware of tuning in, and the difference this makes to the energy in the room. I am looking more at the distortions that may exist in

"One love, one heart, let's get together and feel all right."

BOB MARLEY

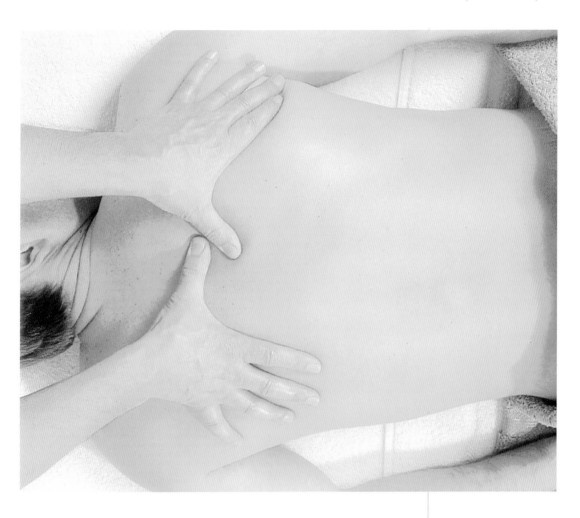

the chakras and energy of the person and am in empathy with the person I am working on.

"When I have time I will use Reiki at the beginning of a session to calm the client down, which gives me a real sense of what they need or what is going on for them. If someone has a specific area of pain during a treatment I will often stop massaging and simply pour Reiki into that area to help move the block. Many of my clients have remarked that they feel more relaxed than when they previously received massage.

"Reiki has been a great asset to me. My advice to other physical therapists who wish to work on a deeper level would be to attend a Reiki course up to second degree, as it would greatly enhance their work."

Above Combining Reiki with deep tissue massage can give a profound sense of security both to the practitioner and the patient.

209

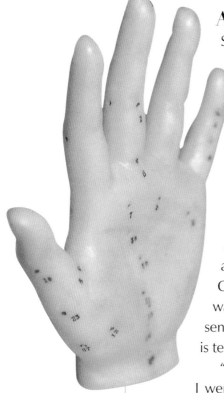

Above Acupuncture utilizes the ki energy within the body and works to redistribute it, creating a deep sense of harmony in the mind, body, and spirit.

Acupuncture

Sue Johnson has been an acupuncturist for over twenty years and is a clinical tutor at the British College of Acupuncture. In 1996 she attended one of my seminars in London.

"As an acupuncturist I often felt that there was more I could be doing to speed up the healing process, rather than just pop in needles and sit back. I wanted to be more involved and would often sit close to the client and talk to them, trying to unearth information that would allow me to gain a greater understanding of their process. A few years after qualifying I went to a seminar by an eminent Chinese doctor, John Shen, who was 86 years old and wanted to pass on some of his vast experience. One sentence stood out from the whole day: 'Acupuncture is ten percent technique and ninety percent spirit.'

"From that day I searched to find out how to 'heal'. I went to many seminars, read many books, and tried many techniques. I was at the point of giving up when Richard (the author) phoned me out of the blue to tell me he wanted to teach me something that would enhance my treatments. That something turned out to be Reiki.

"Acupuncture works by re-balancing the energy already in the body. I often found myself trying to manipulate low levels of energy, spending weeks building up these levels by stimulating the digestive system to draw more from food. By flooding the system with Reiki I can produce changes more rapidly. It is a little like a central heating system. If air gets into the system the radiators are left half-cold. If we release the air by adding more water, the system works again.

"Another hurdle to overcome in treating people with acupuncture is long-held mental and emotional attitudes. These need to be shifted in order for the body to maintain health. These shifts would normally take years, but with Reiki I find these old patterns that have locked themselves inside the structure of the body can be lifted out.

In the past month I have seen three young women in their late twenties with similar gynacological conditions. Interestingly, all three lost their mothers between the ages of ten and fourteen, just the time that the second chakra is developing. Reiki has been of enormous benefit in bringing these old memories and emotions to the surface in order for the healing to take place in their physical bodies."

Below If used in conjunction with Reiki, acupuncture can be an even more effective method of healing. Here, channels are opened in the meridian system using pins.

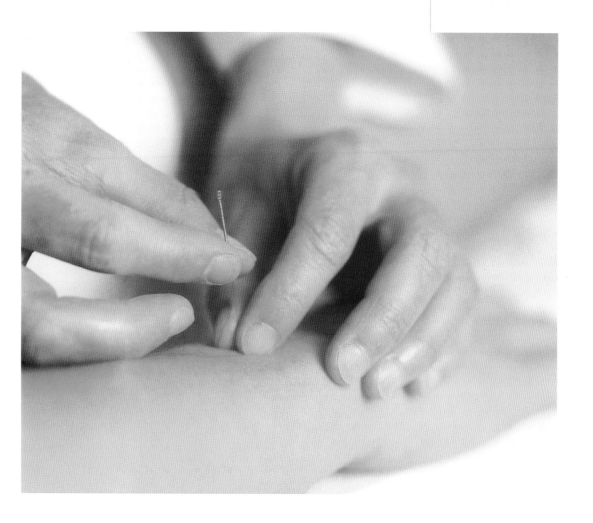

Kirlian Photography Healing Test

For many years healers have talked about their ability to manipulate the energy fields around patients to facilitate healing. The Gas Discharge Visualization machine, cited by Dr. K. Korotkov in Russia, is able to produce a representation of the human energy field utilizing computer, electronic, and optic technology.

Here, we took photographs of a man's energy field before and after a short treatment between photographs for approximately twenty minutes and observed the changes that took place in the field.

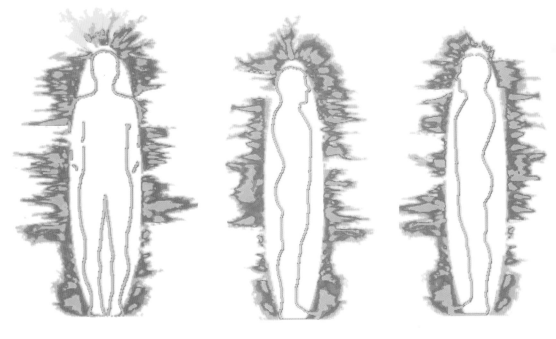

| Front | Right Side | Left Side |

Before Healing (below opposite)

This reveals that the front, left, and right sides of the energy field have strong gaps in the second, third, and fifth chakras. The left emotional side is weaker than the right, and this is reflected in the right side of his brain, with a strong weakness apparent in the field. Generally, the field looks erratic, with areas of both over- and under-activity.

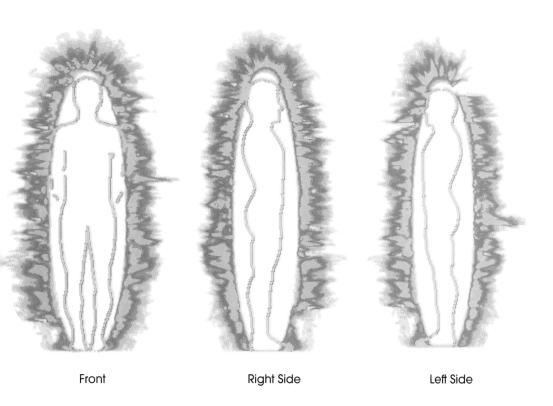

| Front | Right Side | Left Side |

After Healing (above)

After twenty minutes of healing the front, left, and right sides look very different. The gaps that previously existed have disappeared and the overactivity has calmed down. The energy is now in balance and is a good representation of a healthy energy field. The gap in the back of the head in the view of the left side shows where I was still connected physically and demonstrates the importance of disconnecting from the patient after healing.

213

The Origins of Reiki

Reiki has a long and distinguished lineage, which goes right back to the nineteenth century in Japan. It is worth looking at the way the healing technique was developed and how it has been handed down to reach us today. We can greatly enhance our skills of Reiki by looking at its origins.

Above Reiki was born through the vision that Dr. Usui saw while fasting and meditating on the mountain Kuri Yama, near Kyoto, in Japan.

Dr. Mikao Usui

Dr. Mikao Usui, the founder of the Usui system of natural healing, was born in Japan in the mid-nineteenth century. Unfortunately, little is known for certain about the life of Usui beyond his enlightenment on the Reiki healing technique whilst meditating on the sacred mountain Kuri Yama. The most widely accepted source of reliable information on Usui's life is the memorial stone erected by his students, which highlights his experience of "a great Reiki" around his head on Mount Kuri Yama and the healing powers that this gave him. Due to a lack of documented evidence, myth and speculation has grown around Usui's life and teachings.

This is due in part to the late Hawayo Takata, who altered the tale of Dr. Usui to help popularize Reiki in the West. The tale spread by Hawayo Takata begins with Usui living in the city of Kyoto and working as a teacher at a Christian school for boys. During one of his classes he was asked a question that was to change his life: if he believed in the stories told in the Bible of the healing miracles that Jesus performed. Dr. Usui replied that he did. The student replied that he would seek proof of the stories, rather than simply believe what is written in the Bible.

Dr. Usui felt challenged to go out into the world to seek proof of Jesus's healing miracles. His quest took him first to Chicago, where he studied theology and Sanskrit, before returning to Japan seven years later. He finally met an abbot who encouraged him to study the original Buddhist sutras in Sanskrit text. He found mention of methods of healing, but no information that could enable him to activate or access healing energy.

The abbot recommended that he go inward for the answers, through prayer and meditation. Dr. Usui set off on a twenty-one-day fast and retreat on the top of the sacred mountain Kuri Yama, near Kyoto. After climbing the mountain Dr. Usui sat facing east and laid out twenty-one stones before him. Each day he threw a stone away to keep track of the passing days.

In the early hours of the twenty-first day, as he prayed for the answers to his questions, he saw a light moving toward him from across the valley. The light struck him in his third eye (sixth chakra) on the forehead. Dr. Usui was immediately taken into an altered state of color, light, and energy. Symbols, and their meaning, were presented to him, and he was shown how to activate healing energy. He heard the words "Remember remember."

When Dr. Usui awoke from his vision he found it was already light. Despite not eating for twenty-one days he felt full of energy and started running down the mountain. But, in his haste, he fell and cut his toe. He held his foot in his hand and was amazed as his toe was healed after just a few minutes. He continued down the mountain until he came to an inn. On hearing that he had been fasting the proprietor cautioned him against eating, but Dr. Usui ignored him and ate to satisfy his hunger, suffering no indigestion. Dr. Usui then healed the proprietor's granddaughter of toothache by placing his hands on her jaw. Similarly, upon arriving at the monastery and finding the abbot suffering from arthritic pain, Dr. Usui laid his hands on the abbot and the pain went away.

Dr. Usui decided that he would begin working with the new-found energy in the Beggars' Quarter in Kyoto. He lived and worked there every day, treating people by laying his hands on them. He soon realized that, despite the support and encouragement he gave them, people were returning to begging on the streets. When he asked them why, they simply said that it was easier to beg.

Dr. Usui was deeply discouraged by this and chose to lay down the five principles of Reiki. Dr. Usui is said to have initiated sixteen masters in Reiki and he entrusted one of these, Dr. Chujiro Hayashi, to maintain the teachings after his death.

Above Dr. Mikao Usui, founder of the Usui system of natural healing, known throughout the world today as Reiki.

215

Dr. Chujiro Hayashi

Dr. Hayashi was a retired naval officer with a deep interest in spiritual practices. After becoming a Reiki master at the age of forty-seven he opened a clinic in Tokyo and devoted his life to training others in Reiki. His clinic thrived, with practitioners working in groups on patients. Dr. Hayashi established the Reiki positions and the three levels of Reiki, devising an initiation for each level. He was a renowned psychic and, sensing the coming conflict of the Second World War, he felt it important to preserve the knowledge he had been given. He passed the mantle of responsibility to a Japanese woman named Hawayo Takata, living in Hawaii, who had entered his life many years earlier as a patient at his Tokyo clinic.

Above Dr. Chujiro Hayashi, founder of the first Reiki clinic in Tokyo, Japan, developed the hand positions and the three levels of Reiki.

Hawayo Takata

Born on the island of Kauai on December 24 1900, Hawayo Takata's parents were Japanese immigrants, her father working in the sugar cane fields. She married Saichi Takata, the bookkeeper for the plantation, and they had two daughters. Saichi died in 1930, leaving Mrs. Takata to raise their children.

Life was not easy for Hawayo and she had to work hard to provide for her family. She developed nervous exhaustion and severe abdominal pain. Soon after, one of her sisters died and Hawayo traveled to Japan to deliver the news to her parents. While there her condition deteriorated and she went to hospital. It was found that she had a tumor, gallstones, and appendicitis. She needed an operation.

While being prepared for the anaesthetic Hawayo heard a voice, which told her that the operation was not necessary. She knew she was wide awake, and had not imagined the voice, but had not experienced anything like this before. She asked a doctor if he knew of any other way that she could be healed. The doctor told her about Dr. Hayashi's Reiki clinic.

On visiting the clinic Hawayo was impressed by the Reiki practitioner's ability to detect problem areas simply by scanning the body with his hands. The heat from his hands was so strong that she believed he must be using some sort of equipment and tried to grab the sleeves of his kimono to see what he was concealing. The practitioner was startled, but once Hawayo explained her misgivings, he began to laugh. He told her about Reiki and how it worked.

Above Hawayo Takata discovered the Reiki system when she was treated by Dr. Chujiro Hayashi.

Mrs. Takata received daily treatments and her condition improved. In four months she was completely healed. She was impressed with these results and wanted to learn Reiki. In the spring of 1936, Mrs. Takata received first degree Reiki and she worked with Dr. Hayashi for one year before receiving second degree Reiki.

Mrs. Takata returned to Hawaii in 1937 and was initiated as a Reiki master by Dr. Hayashi soon after. He then announced that he wished her to be his successor.

Hawayo Takata somehow escaped incarceration as a Japanese American during the Second World War. By the time of her death on December 11 1980, she had initiated twenty-two Reiki masters. She named Phyllis Lei Furumoto, her granddaughter, as her successor.

217

The Five Spiritual Principles of Reiki

These principles were put in place by Dr. Mikao Usui, the founder of the Usui system of natural healing, shortly after he had been working with beggars on the streets of Kyoto. He had decided that he needed to give guidelines to the people he worked with in order for them to live a more fulfilled life. The guidelines constitute ways in which we can take more responsibility for our lives and, although they were written over one hundred years ago, they are still relevant today.

Just for Today do not Worry

This principle reminds us that we must trust in the process of life. When we worry, it is often because we have become caught in the confusion of our outer experience and have become fearful of the future. Our fear leads us to attempt to control all aspects of our lives, rather than trusting in the natural abundance and security that comes from being in our natural place. When we worry we send our fears out into the world, and when the world reflects them the spiral of confusion gains momentum in our lives. Instead, try to relax and know that what is yours will come to you at the right time.

Just for Today do not Anger

When we feel anger it is often because we have given away our power, or failed in some way to express our needs. The outer world is a reflection, so if we find ourselves angry with someone they are often only doing us a service and showing us what needs attention in our own lives. We are, in fact, angry with ourselves for failing to take the action that would have prevented the situation arising in the first place.

Honor your Parents, Teachers, and Elders

It is easy to lay the blame for all that is wrong in our lives at the door of our parents, teachers, or elders. If we are able to rise up and see life from a greater perspective, then we can realize that everyone in our lives is there for a reason. Those who give us the greatest lessons are those who love us the most. It is important to recognize that nothing happens by chance: you have chosen your parents and your life situation in order to experience the very difficulties you need to grow. Love them and honor them for being part of your experience.

Earn your Living Honestly

Through our work we express ourselves. When we receive payment for what we do we learn to respect ourselves and take responsibility for our lives. It is important that we find our place in the world and express our unique gifts.

Show Gratitude to Everything

Never take anything for granted. Instead, give thanks for every meal you eat, every day you live, every prayer that is answered. Life is so very precious and, as we learn to appreciate our own life, we will learn to appreciate all life.

Resource Directory

The Reiki Association
www.reikiassociation.org.uk

The Reiki Alliance
www.reikialliance.com

Reiki Outreach International
www.reikioutreach.com

International Association of Reiki Professionals
www.iarp.org

Canadian Reiki Association
Box 54570
7155 Kingsway
Burnaby , BC
V5E 4J6
www.reiki.ca

Australian Reiki Connection Inc.
ARC Inc.
PO Box 525
MONBULK
VIC 3793
Australia
www.australianreikiconnection.
   com.au

The International Center for Reiki Training
21421 Hilltop Street,
Unit #28, Southfield,
Michigan 48033 USA
www.reiki.org

Index

Page numbers in **bold** refer to illustrations

Index

Credits

Quantum Publishing Ltd. would like to thank and acknowledge the following for providing pictures reproduced in this book:

Corbis: 170
Image Bank 26, 103, 111, 203
iStock: 219
Richard Ellis 45
Shutterstock: 13, 15, 18, 28, 32, 35, 37, 39, 40, 43, 47, 57, 70, 92, 98, 113, 119, 121, 123, 125, 129, 131, 133, 134, 135, 136, 137, 138, 139, 140, 141, 142, 145, 147, 149, 150, 153, 155,159, 160, 163, 164, 173, 174, 177, 178, 181, 182, 185, 186, 189, 193, 194, 204

The photographs on pages 215, 216 and 217 are reproduced with the permission of Phyllis Lei Furumoto.

All other photographs and illustrations are the copyright of Quantum Publishing Ltd

While every effort has been made to credit contributors, Quantum would like to apologize should there have been any omissions or errors.